CHILDREN OF
THE MONSOON

CHILDREN OF THE MONSOON

David Jiménez

Translated by Andrea Rosenberg

Bloomington, Indiana & Iowa City, Iowa

This is an Autumn Hill Books book
Published by Autumn Hill Books, Inc.
1138 E. Benson Court
Bloomington, Indiana 47401

Printed in the United States of America

Cover photograph of "Chuan the Invincible" by David Jiménez

Design and layout by Xavier Comas
Proofreading by Michael Wykoff

Autumn Hill Books ISBN: 978-0-9827466-7-7
Library of Congress Control Number: 2013939375

www.autumnhillbooks.org

To Carmen

Contents

Vothy

Not four seasons but two. Dry. Wet.

The house where I stayed on my last trip sat on a vast expanse of thirsty soil; now it is hemmed in by water in the middle of a wide pool. The rains have painted the dying landscape of withered palms and parched rice paddies with the impossible greens of a watercolor. The river carrying me south—wasn't it a stony dirt road just a few months ago? You travel to a country during the dry season, and when you return during the monsoon, you no longer recognize it. It is transformed. The magic of the seasons is repeated every year east of the Suez, where the days break first and the Sky God decides which dreams will come true this season.

And which will have to wait until the next.

The monsoon is everything in Asia. People wait for it with impatience, with longing—and with dread. It gives life and takes it away. It can arrive early enough to halt a military offensive in the jungles of Burma, or bring famine to millions of Indian peasants if it's late. Sometimes it floods eveything in its path, erasing borders that haven't always existed. This complicates things for the soldiers charged with defending the nation, since they can't tell where their territory begins or ends. The line that separates them from the others lies underwater, and they may confuse a boat full of soldiers from a neighboring country struggling to stay afloat with an enemy incursion. Are they on their side of the line or on ours? Do we help them, or shoot them?

The magic of the seasons pulls off its most amazing trick in the Mekong. The "river of evil memory" is born in Tibet, where the shepherds believe a mighty dragon guards its source to make sure it will never stop flowing, as its waters are considered the blood that runs through the veins of the people who live on its banks. Without it, life would not be possible. After leaving China, the river grows murky as it passes through the heart of Southeast Asia, becoming for much of its length an endless fount the color of milky coffee, perhaps to hide old betrayals, the colonial atrocities and devastating wars that have done so much harm to its peoples. Winding through jungles and valleys, the Mekong traces the border between Burma and Thailand, passes through Laos and Cambodia, and finally dies, full of life, in Vietnam.

The Tonlé Sap, one of the river's tributaries, flows southwest through Cambodia when there are no rains, but during the monsoon its waters abruptly rise and reverse course, flowing northward into Lake Tonlé. Only when the rains come to an end does it take up once more its usual course toward the South China Sea. The miracle of the Mekong's reversal is celebrated throughout the country with a large festival and fireworks. It is the beginning of the wedding season.

With people's hearts in tumult, matchmakers go from town to town acting as go-betweens and arranging marriages for a small commission, based on the terms negotiated between the families and the number of sacks of rice a suitor can offer. The elder members of the community say that it's always been this way and that traditions should be respected. But the only tradition that never dies in the villages of the Cambodian countryside is poverty, which makes love a prized asset, the only asset. Only a fool would just give it away.

Kong Thai and Touh Sokgan broke the rules and gave theirs away. He was a scrawny man, teeth rotting and tobacco-stained, hair grimy, with a wife and four children from an earlier, unsuccessful life. His best years had been left behind in the rice paddies, and they weren't coming back. She'd been the most sought-after young woman in the village, her skin browned by the tropical sun, with high cheekbones, soft lips, and ebony hair. She was supposed to marry someone who owned at least one plot of land and half a dozen animals, but ignored her family's objections to a man they said would bring nothing but trouble. Sokgan and Thai decided to abandon the life of the monsoon, tired of waiting for the rains in the years it arrived late, and tired of wishing it had never come in those years when it unleashed its fury upon the village. They came together, in defiance of everything and everybody, in their tiny village in Svay Rieng province near the Vietnamese border, and left to live out their improbable dream in the capital city.

In Phnom Penh they found the same lodging that all newcomers do: a room, a rickety bed, a fan, a window, and plenty of rats, all for a dollar a day. Sokgan took care of the house during the day, while Thai took a job as a rickshaw driver. At the time, you could accurately assess how the country was doing by the number of rickshaws in the city. The more rickshaws there were, the more destitute trying to make ends meet. When Kong Thai started his new job at the beginning of the '90s, there were thousands of trishaws in Phnom Penh, driven to and fro by peasants newly arrived from the countryside, war veterans who still had both their legs, lunatics, and unfortunates of all stripes. Cambodia had been shattered by decades of invasions, bombings, civil war, and Pol Pot's genocide. Its people didn't know it yet, but just as they were starting to recover from those old wounds, a new, silent tragedy had begun to strike at the heart of Cambodian society. AIDS had slipped silently into the lives of those charged with the task of pulling the nation out of its deep well of misery.

Sokgan has never understood how that scrawny, feeble man who promised her a new life in the city could have the strength after an arduous workday to pedal another eleven kilometers to the brothels of Svay Pak, on the outskirts of the city, to spend his day's earnings there. But it's too late now for regrets. She is lying naked, too weak to feign modesty about the body she no longer recognizes as her own, in a room on the third floor of the Russian hospital in Phnom Penh. The young woman has watched her own beauty gradually decay, washed away like a watercolor in the rain. Her breasts have shrunk and disappeared, her face has flattened, her thighs have grown thin and her voice weak; she spends the nights howling. She can't remember the last time she looked in a mirror. When I see her huddled there on the rickety bed, motionless, I hesitate in the doorway. Is she alive? Is she dead? Only her bones remain and, folded over them, piles of extra skin, languid, unfixed, looking at any moment as if they might slide off her body and leave her skeleton bare.

Thai must have brought AIDS into the house almost immediately, because Vothy, their daughter, was also born with HIV. There's an old suitcase under the bed that mother and daughter share in the Russian hospital, the kind of old perfume salesman would carry, rectangular, made of brown artificial leather with metal corners, battered and slightly pompous. Everything they own is in that suitcase. Vothy's pink dress, her mother's blue dress; Vothy's pair of patent-leather shoes, her mother's sandals; Vothy's earrings, her mother's earrings; a small brush for Vothy, a big one for her mother.

Sokgan had refused to go to the hospital, figuring that if she was going to die, it made no difference where she did it. In any case, every day she had less strength for the trip and so always put it off till tomorrow tomorrow tomorrow . . . Only when she found the first lesions on her daughter's skin, lesions like the ones that for her had signaled the beginning of the end, did she muster what was left of her strength, stare her husband down with the full force of her pent-up rage, and demand that he take the two of them to the hospital. You and I might die tomorrow, and it might even have been better if we'd died already, but how is it Vothy's fault that you spent your rickshaw money in the Svay Pak brothels? And don't bother lying to me anymore. The doctor said AIDS can't be transmitted through food or water, only through weakness, which you've always had in spades.

So Kong Thai pedaled the fifteen kilometers between the family's room—the rickety old bed with its fan, window, and rats, all for a dollar—and the hospital, his daughter and wife clutching their suitcase in the rear of the rickshaw, sobbing. The sick were lined up at the hospital entrance, lying on the ground, too weak to stand, waiting for today's dead to make room for the dead of tomorrow. They waited there for hours until, as night fell, a nurse called them and began the admissions process. At the top of the form she wrote the date:

AUGUST 22, 2000.
Name: TOUH SOKGAN.
Age: 27 YEARS.
Symptoms: SKIN LESIONS, NAUSEA, VOMITING, WEIGHT
LOSS, COUGH, ULCERS.
Weight: 28 KG.
Condition: TERMINAL AIDS.

Name: KONG VOTHY.
Age: 5 YEARS.
Symptoms: SKIN LESIONS, NAUSEA, HAIR LOSS.
Weight: 17 KG.
Condition: (Probably) AIDS.

Sokgan was embarrassed by the questions about her sexual history, offended that she'd been taken for a prostitute. She said her only sexual partner had been a rickshaw driver. Even though at the time many housewives were contracting the disease from their husbands, doctors identified any woman they diagnosed with AIDS as a prostitute. AIDS was a whores' disease, not a disease of the johns who visited them.

Finally, the nurse asked the two new patients if they had any family. This was important, she said, because if the parents died before their daughter and left her an orphan—a likely scenario—the hospital would take her to the village of her extended family, as the staff had found that a grandparent, uncle, or cousin was always willing to take in a child.

Family: NONE.
Family: NONE.

The Cambodians call Preah Sihanouk "the Russian hospital" because it was built during the Soviet era with money from Moscow. The AIDS ward occupies a building set apart from the rest of the hospital. It is the only one that has a budget for feeding its patients. In the other wards, family members of the patients are responsible for providing food, but here most of the patients have nobody and so the hospital must give them something to eat. After setting aside some funds to compensate himself for the inconveniences of his job, the accountant distributes the rest with scrupulous impartiality. This month: twelve cents per patient per day. According to the accountant, it's more than enough. AIDS patients don't have much of an appetite, so there's no reason to spend a lot feeding them. Nor is it necessary to treat them—since none of them can be saved. Even the doctors are afraid of catching the disease and hardly ever come by; the nurses, who earn a pittance—even less than the accountant and the doctors—only cover their shifts if they have nothing better to do that day. The place is simply the antechamber to the cemetery, where ailing patients are expected to die as quickly as possible and without bothering anybody else.

I wait for Sokgan to make some movement to confirm that she's still alive before I enter the room. My first question—how is she doing?—is a dumb one, and she answers with a keen wail, almost a shout. Tears mean a lot more in a place where people rarely cry. From the cradle, children are taught that crying won't do much good. It did not help adults either during the genocide.

Sokgan gestures for me to come closer.

"The girl," she mutters, clinging to my neck, "nobody will want her. She has AIDS. Do you understand? She doesn't have anybody."

Vothy enters the room a few seconds later, dries her mother's tears, hands her a glass of water, and hops to her feet. She presses her palms together in front of her chest and bows in the traditional Cambodian greeting.

"Are you a foreigner from America?" she asks.

Unlike her mother, there's light in her eyes. During the long, tedious afternoons, when everything is desolation, on those days when the patients seem to have realized that they are all alone and will leave the hospital the same way they arrived—with nothing—Vothy puts on her pink dress and goes from room to room, dancing, bringing food to the patients, and telling them all that yes, she also has that thing called AIDS, and there's nothing to worry about, because they're safe now in the hospital. And if somebody's room is suddenly left empty, Vothy recounts how that patient has gotten better and gone back home. Perhaps it is in part because of the way she repeats this lie her mother has told her so many times that the other patients feel such tenderness toward her. No one could say for sure, but everyone suspects that Vothy knows there's no hope for any of them. She has to have seen the nurses carrying out the corpses, smelled the whiff of death that drifts down the corridors from time to time, heard the mothers weeping over the loss of their daughters. And yet everybody pretends to believe her tales of survival—if only to make sure she visits them again. The bond with the girl grows stronger as the patients get weaker. At first the certainty of death causes them to resist getting close to others, but when the final journey has begun, they cling to any affection, however small. They call Vothy's name from the corridor, asking her to come talk to them; they bicker over having her stay a little longer. It's hard to believe that the last breath of life in the Russian hospital is a five-year-old girl.

Vothy has been taking care of her mother ever since they arrived at the hospital. Every day she cooks rice for her, washes her clothes, and helps her dress her skeletal frame. Her father, Kong Thai, comes by occasionally with a bag of mangos for dinner, waits for Vothy to fall asleep, and then makes love to what's left of his wife. Tun, a young Cambodian woman with a soft voice and long, straight hair who runs a nursery on the ground floor of the hospital, curses in Khmer whenever she sees Thai in the corridor.

"He looks so ill now, they won't let him into the brothels anymore," says Tun, her sweetness shot through with anger for a moment. "So he comes here to sleep with his wife, even though she can barely stand. She lets him do it and doesn't object, because that's how women are brought up in Cambodia."

The walls of Tun's nursery are covered with the artwork of children who have passed away. When she accepted the position offered by the NGO, Friends International, Tun believed it would be just another job. And yet here she is, constantly picking up the pieces of her shattered heart. She has decided to fight to keep Vothy alive to the very end in the hope that the latest medicines to treat AIDS will arrive in Cambodia in time to save her. Every week she takes her to the Kantha Bopha Children's Hospital in Phnom Penh to see Dr. Beat Richner. The Swiss doctor is the only one who can give her the vitamins to boost her immune system and prevent an infection from finishing her off within days. Twice a week Tun and Vothy climb into a rickshaw and cross the city to Dr. Richner's hospital. Vothy enjoys the trips, waving to people on the street and buying a sweet before returning to the Russian hospital.

"There are people like you there," she tells me.

"People like me?"

"Yes, foreigners. Doctors with big noses."

When it comes time for me to leave, Vothy asks when I'll be back. I hadn't planned on it, but I promise to come for another visit after a trip to the north of the country before flying back to Hong Kong. Five days later I'm in the room on the third floor once more. Sokgan is still in her bed—dead? alive?—but Vothy isn't with her. She appears soon after, running down the hall with other children in hot pursuit and laughing as they shout, "Don't run, Baldy, don't run, we're going to catch you!" Tun gave her the nickname. One day, seeing the little girl eyeing herself sadly in the mirror, Tun decided to take her to a hairdresser so she could get her head shaved and hide the hair loss the illness had caused. It was that day, perhaps, that Tun and Vothy had become inseparable.

I lift my camera to take a photo of Vothy as she runs toward me, but when she's a couple of meters away she stops short and covers her eyes with her hands.

"Just a minute," she says. "Let me put on my pink dress."

She enters the room where her mother lies, wriggles under the bed, and pulls out the old traveling-salesman suitcase. She grabs the ruffled pink dress, the special-occasion dress, lifts it over her head, and lets it fall slowly around her, twisting her shoulders and hips to adjust it. Finally she ties the bow at the back and says, "Ready!"

Several years would pass before I'd return to this place with that photograph in my hand and ask after the little girl in the pink dress, hoping those medicines that were saving so many people's lives in the West had arrived in time to rescue Vothy and the rest of this country's people, who have been betrayed so many times.

Too often the fates of countries that don't matter are decided halfway around the world by countries that do. The people's lives are determined even before they are born, through a chain of circumstances and events that gradually shape their future, so that any attempt they later make to change it is of little use. Their futures have been defined by politicians who have never been to the places whose fates they're deciding. These leaders could never understand these faraway people's situation or put themselves in their place; they have never stopped to think about the consequences of their actions in the lives of actual human beings thousands of kilometers from their comfortable offices. Cambodia is one such place, a country inhabited by a people whose destiny has been stolen from them.

The deciding of Cambodia's future beyond its borders first began when the United States stuck its oar in, supporting the coup that brought down Prince Norodom Sihanouk and bombing the countryside in an effort to destroy alleged guerrilla encampments during the Vietnam War. The American attacks meant thousands of new recruits for the Communist guerrilla forces led by the as yet unknown Soloth Sar, who would later enter the history books as one of the great mass murderers of the twentieth century, Pol Pot. Brother Number One marched triumphant into Phnom Penh in 1975, accompanied by the cheers of the war-weary populace. He declared it Year Zero, the beginning of everything, and began to transform the country into a proletarian paradise. The urban population was sent to the countryside, the country's economy was dismantled after the model Mao had used to bring China to ruin, and the ideological purification of Kampuchea began. Money, postal mail, and newspapers were abolished. Having a university education, speaking a foreign language, wearing glasses, or dressing immodestly became reason enough to be sent to a forced labor camp. According to Pol Pot, only pure peasants would be able to carry out his revolutionary vision. Angkar, the party organization that was established to control the country, denounced everybody else with a simple slogan: "To keep you is no benefit. To destroy you is no loss."

Thousands of children were taken to communist re-education camps, trained in hatred, and recruited to serve a regime that sometimes tested their loyalty by forcing them to execute their own families. About 1.7 million people died throughout the country, a record for genocidal speed and efficiency. At the time, Cambodia had only seven million inhabitants, and the Khmer Rouge was only in power three years, eight months, and twenty days. Even today when I visit Cambodia, I do a little test that never fails—and that never fails to surprise me. I choose a person at random—the porter at the hotel, the waiter at the restaurant, the saleswoman at the photo shop—and I ask for their story of the genocide. And everyone has a personal story of the genocide to tell: one or more family members who died in prison, a son who disappeared, the memory of an execution, long years of hunger and torture in forced labor camps. The Cambodian genocide, unlike the ones that came before and after it, unlike the Holocaust or Rwanda, was not directed against a religion, an ethnicity, or any specific group. The Cambodians exterminated themselves; they autogenocided. Brother against brother, friend against friend, killing each other over ideas that many of them never really understood. That they still don't understand.

With the invasion of Vietnam's army in 1978, the madness of Pol Pot came to an end and a painful occupation began. China and the United States both—but for opposing reasons—supported Pol Pot's retreating guerrilla army; they dragged out the civil war and for a number of years left open the possibility of Angkar's return. In one of history's greatest instances of political cynicism, the flag of Khmer Rouge Cambodia, the banner of the killing fields, still waved over the entrance of the United Nations in New York. For the Western powers, there was nothing odd about making a pact with the devil: the enemy of their enemy (Vietnam) was their friend, even if he'd been responsible for Asia's Holocaust. A fragile peace was finally established only in 1991. Soon after, twenty-two thousand soldiers and civil officials from the United Nations Transitional Authority in Cambodia (UNTAC) began patrolling the streets of the capital. The

Cambodians couldn't believe their luck. Could it be real? All those people from so far away come just to help them?

One of the first things foreign troops did upon arriving in Cambodia was to create brothels to service the barracks. They filled them with young women from the poor neighborhoods of the capital city, women for whom the proffered dollars were an opportunity to rescue their families from poverty. The UNTAC soldiers gradually expanded the network of brothels. Each unit wanted one of its own—there were participants from more than thirty countries, from Cameroon to New Zealand, from Bulgaria to the United States—and soldiers demonstrated their camaraderie by inviting soldiers from allied countries to try out their brothel. The soldiers, police officers, and UN officials got drunk, brawled in the bars, urinated in the temples, and assaulted the Cambodians, enjoying the impunity they'd been granted. Some had come with the best of intentions, but their mission inevitably turned into a circus. Everyone wanted to have a good time, and if what you wanted was to have a good time without having to explain yourself to anybody or worry about the consequences, there was no better place for it than broken Cambodia.

News of the arrival of foreign dollars traveled quickly among the desperately poor, and families began knocking on the doors of the military bases and offering their daughters. Once a person has nothing else of value left—when only dignity remains—then dignity, too, has its price. On my first trip to Cambodia, walking through the streets of Phnom Penh, I crossed paths with a woman leading her daughter by the hand. The girl couldn't have been older than thirteen.

"Ten dollars," she told me, while the girl hung her head.

I thought she was asking for charity. Then the mother uncovered her daughter's still undeveloped breasts right there in the street and repeated, "Ten dollars, mister, and she's yours."

The UN troops that came to Cambodia were only continuing the age-old tradition that has brought together mass prostitution in Southeast Asia and military testosterone ever since American soldiers made the Thai village of Pattaya their destination of choice when they went on leave during the Vietnam War. Prostitution, of course, had always existed in those places, but the soldiers laid the foundations for a whole industry built on exploitation, dramatically increasing the number of young women willing to enter the business and leaving a legacy that has persisted long after they packed their duffle bags and returned to base. The industry has grown so much that today it requires a constant supply of new young women, since once they hit twenty-two they are considered "antiques" and are retired from the marketplace and replaced with others. On my trips through the years, I have seen how the merchandise on offer in the doorways of some Asian discotheques is constantly updated. Little girls I first saw begging outside a shop end up offering themselves a few years later. I especially remember a mute girl who used to sell flowers outside the Apocalypse Now, one of the trendy nightclubs in Saigon. The first time I met her, she was just ten years old. Every year she grew a little taller. And then one day she was not at the entrance to the club. I found her inside on the dance floor, dressed in a denim miniskirt and a yellow top. She had a tattoo on her back. She was holding a cigarette in one hand and a beer in the other. A tourist had slipped his arm around her narrow waist and was pressing her against his beer belly. The little flower girl now silently sold nights of feigned passion to men with whom she couldn't speak—and to whom, in any case, she had nothing to say.

What made the UN soldiers who came to Cambodia different was that a large part of the multinational force now carousing in the tropics was made up of soldiers from African nations that were being ravaged by AIDS. The virus was soon passed on to the Cambodian girls who showed up at the barracks, and then to their boyfriends, their friends, their villages. Thousands of young women who came to the big city to earn money for their families returned to their villages, harboring not only the secret of having worked as something besides a hotel maid but also an illness they'd never even heard of. For those women, the greatest shame was not in renting themselves by the hour but in returning empty-handed, in not being able to pay for their young siblings' education or an ailing grandmother's medicines. In their villages, people could tell which families had daughters who'd been able to save enough, because they lived in cement houses with wells and even electricity, symbols of success that inspired younger generations to try their luck, too.

Unlimited supply.

In the Kantha Bopha Children's Hospital in Phnom Penh, Dr. Beat Richner was one of the first to detect, in 1993, that the AIDS virus was spreading through the Cambodian population. The Swiss doctor had arrived in the country for the first time in 1974, when he was still in his twenties, and started volunteering at Bopha Hospital. He was forced to flee a year later when the Khmer Rouge seized power. He returned in 1991 to find the hospital in ruins, and decided to stay and rebuild it. These days the doctor plays the cello beside the river of evil memory, gives fundraising concerts around the world, and takes care of sick children at any of the three hospitals he runs in Cambodia. The world, Dr. Richner likes to say, has become another *Titanic*, where the doors of the third-class passengers' cabins are locked so that the first-class passengers can be saved.

It didn't take long for Richner to link the country's AIDS epidemic with the soldiers, and he decided to contact UN administrators in an effort to make them aware of the situation. On numerous occasions he requested that they compel soldiers to use condoms and recommended they all be tested to find out which ones were carrying the virus. The chief of mission, Yasushi Akashi, responded that the soldiers' behavior was perfectly understandable: they were far from home and had the right to have a good time every once in a while. His answer, in short: "Boys will be boys." In 1991, before the arrival of international troops for what was to that point the largest and most costly operation in United Nations history, Cambodian health authorities had detected only a single case of AIDS in the whole country. Before the decade's end, four percent of the population was infected, two hundred people were contracting the virus each day, the country had the most serious AIDS epidemic in all of Asia, and thousands of kids were working as prostitutes in the capital city. By then, the soldiers were long gone. Tourists and especially locals, who, despite a widespread misconception, are consumers of much of the sex industry in Southeast Asia, had taken up the baton and become the latest customers.

Unlimited demand, too.

The events that had brought Vothy to the Russian hospital in Phnom Penh had begun in the offices of negligent politicians. Her future had been shaped by a series of betrayals. One of the two most recent betrayals was that of the foreigners who had won the Cambodian people's trust and arrived with the mission of helping the country, only to bequeath the ravaged nation a new legacy of death. The other was that of the man who at the end of his workdays kept pedaling his rickshaw until he reached the brothels of Svay Pak.

I first heard about Svay Pak from Vichea, who'd been my inseparable guide in Cambodia ever since I first met him outside the Hotel Princess in Phnom Penh in 1998. Today, with the passing of the years, I can no longer picture the Phnom Penh airport without seeing him smiling as he clears a path through the people who crowd around the main entrance to the airport even though they have no one to wait for, massing near the door out of curiosity or because they've got nothing better to do, and hearing him say in English, as if it were the first time we met, "Welcome, Mr. David."

The story of Vichea's courage is the sort of story you usually find in those countries where nobody gives anything for free. As a boy he pedaled a rickshaw like Kong Thai's for seven years, gradually saving enough to buy a motorcycle, which he used to carry passengers around the city until he managed to get a loan to buy a car and become a taxi driver. Despite his fifteen-hour workdays, he invested part of his money in English classes and now speaks the language better than most of the foreigners he drives around. After his English classes, he took up studying Mandarin, because the future, he'd always say, is in the Chinese tourists who are all over the place now.

The day Vichea mentioned Svay Pak, he had called the hotel to tell me he was going to be late. A customer had taken longer than expected at the "chicken farm."

"Does he raise chickens?" I asked.

"No, man," said Vichea, laughing. "Chicks, girls, you know."

The next day we traveled the eleven kilometers to Svay Pak. At the entrance was an enormous sign welcoming customers in eight different languages: "We love safe sex. Please use condoms." Every single house in the village had been turned into a brothel. As we walked down the street, the sliding doors of what must have once been private residences and shops opened on either side of us, revealing young girls disguised as women. None of them were through puberty yet, but they were smeared with rouge, dressed in provocative patent-leather and vinyl clothing, all of them swaying suggestively and calling out to visitors the only English sentences they'd learned: "Hey, mister, mister, short time? Have fun."

Back then, Svay Pak was the only place in Cambodia where the country's brutal social differences went unnoticed. Rich men and poor, foreign and local, handsome and ugly, tall and short, shared the same dim rooms, dealt with the same pimps, and watched the girls parade before them with the same anxious expression on their faces until finally choosing the one they liked best. The owners adjusted their prices depending on the client. They were as happy to accept the three dollars that a man like Kong Thai could afford for one of their twenty-two-year-old "antiques" as they were to demand five hundred dollars from the Westerners and Asians who'd show up with special requests, a "real virgin" and not one of those girls who'd just had her hymen reconstructed.

Cambodia was now the country in which immoral behavior had become acceptable simply because it was possible. Phnom Penh had become a haven for fugitive criminals, assassins, pimps, mercenaries, and family men in the throes of a midlife crisis. They had all come because of an urgent need to hide themselves away somewhere where nobody could reproach them for their deeds. Broken nations can be the perfect therapy. In the restaurants, they treat you like a prime minister just for being white, and gorgeous girls who wouldn't even look at you in your country smile at you on the street. It may be hell for the locals, but for you it's paradise. The ne'er-do-wells of the world had found their playground. They called Svay Pak Sexyland because anything went in its brothels, no matter how perverse, and nothing was really illegal, either: the police officers, public officials, and political leaders supposedly responsible for upholding the law were out there as well, waiting their turn. Then there was Disney War, a firing range set up by Cambodian soldiers near the airport, where you could hurl a grenade or fire an AK-47 at a cow in exchange for a few dollars. And Potland, a place where getting high was so easy that Sophol and Vi, a delightful Cambodian couple, had opened a restaurant beside the river called Happy Herb Pizza whose pizzas even today are served "happy" or "very happy," depending how much marijuana is in the crust.

"The customer always comes back," Sophol told me, laughing, the day her happy pizza sent me back to my hotel room for a nap.

Vichea is waiting for me in the airport as usual. It's been a couple of years since my last visit and four since I met Vothy in the Russian hospital. On the way to the hotel, Vichea tells me all the latest news. His mother has returned home after spending five years in religious seclusion in a Buddhist monastery, where she'd gone after she found her husband with another woman significantly younger than herself. Now that she was back, she had asked Vichea to marry a friend's daughter, who had a fairly modest dowry: 650 dollars.

"After the trouble she had with my father, I couldn't refuse to let her choose a wife for me. So I said yes. Now I have a family."

Every two or three months, Vichea, his wife, and his newborn son get into a taxi and go through the city in search of a place to live. When they find one, they rent it and move in, and then resignedly await the arrival of the rats. They block all the holes and put out rat poison, but Vichea suspects the poison must be made of some sort of rodent delicacy, because there are more and more of them all the time, he buys more and more poison, and the man who sells it to him makes more and more money. When the rats get to be too much for them, Vichea, his wife, and their son get back into the car, go through the city, and look for another room: a rickety old bed, a fan, a window, and plenty of rats, all of it, for a dollar a day.

It saddens me to see how Vichea's efforts to get himself and his family out of poverty have been fruitless. It is only possible to feel the humiliation of failure if we have first allowed the expectation of success to grow within us. Only when we invest our pride and our energy into a goal we never reach do we feel the frustration of not achieving it. For a peasant who's known nothing but rural life, who hopes for nothing more than a good harvest and a daughter who marries well before she turns sixteen, life in a country like Cambodia will always be hard. But it's even harder for men like Vichea. He is part of that minority of people who possess a strong work ethic, intelligence, an entrepreneurial spirit, and all those things that in a land of opportunities would have made him successful. But this is the land of no opportunities, a place where personal worth does not matter. In Cambodia, when you apply for a job as a government official, you know they're going to give it to another official's cousin. Corruption is so entrenched in the system, and so accepted, that you can tell which villages the ministers' mothers live in because the roads leading to them are the only ones that are paved.

The next-to-last day of the month is envelope day. Vichea has to give one to his son's teacher at school so his son doesn't get beaten, another to the utilities man so they don't cut his electricity on Saturday nights, and another to the security guards at the airport so they'll allow him to pick up passengers with his taxi. Driving along Chairman Mao Road near the Hotel Intercontinental, we encounter a police checkpoint. They want to search the car.

"They're looking for illegal weapons," Vichea explains. "If the policemen find a gun, they go sell it on the black market. The gun's former owner needs a new one, so he goes to the black market, looks in a few different stalls, spots a gun he likes. It looks a lot like the one he had. 'Wow,' he says, 'that's my gun. What's it doing here?' He buys it again, until the police stop his car at another checkpoint . . ."

Vichea is able to describe the contradictions in his country with a peculiar sort of black humor shared by many other Cambodians, which over time I've come to understand as an antidote to despair. But the Vichea who has come to meet me this time is not the same one I've seen on other occasions: his strength to swim against the current is flagging. His humor has turned bitter. He takes me to the Friendship Bridge, a gift from the Japanese, and stops the car. "See that police boat?" he says. "It's there twenty-four hours a day to pick up desperate young women who are tired of selling themselves in the brothels, or taxi drivers like me who aren't going to make it to the end of the month. People decide to throw themselves into the river. But it looks bad for the government, so the boat rushes out and picks you up before you can drown. They bring you back to life. We don't even own our own lives."

At night we go to Phnom Penh's Foreign Correspondents Club, a colonial building where you can still run into the photographer Al Rockoff, who was played by John Malkovich in The Killing Fields, one of the best film portrayals of the Cambodian genocide. Through the windows we can see lights on the river, fishing boats headed downstream now that the rains have stopped and the current has turned back toward the South China Sea. We reminisce about old adventures and the stories Vichea has helped me write, about that time in the Russian hospital. I show him the photograph of Vothy I've brought with me.

"Yes, I remember her," Vichea says. "She was a special little girl. I didn't want to go into the hospital that day, I was really scared, I didn't know if AIDS could be transmitted through the air. Now everybody knows you have to put on a condom before you boom-boom. We Cambodians use two, because the ones they make here are really cheap and they break easily."

"What happened to her?"

"I never went back to that place. She probably died. This country is a shithole, you know. The other day, my son caught dengue. He almost died on me because none of the hospitals wanted to give him medicine unless I paid them in advance. I had to put on the only jacket I own and pretend to be rich so they'd let me into the emergency ward. And we're talking about a public hospital. Either you go to the Swiss doctor's place, or your child dies without anybody caring."

"We'll go see her tomorrow."

"Who?"

"The little girl in the pink dress."

I have come and gone so many times, to so many places, in such a hurry, that sometimes it feels like I've been in most of them without really being. My first years as a correspondent in Asia passed quickly, tinged with a persistent impatience to see a new place, cover another conflict, file another report, get another stamp in my passport. I might begin the week in Japan and end it in Pakistan, describe five-year-old children breaking rocks in Bangladesh on Monday and on Friday discuss the latest rise of the Hong Kong stock exchange. With the years, that rushed journalism—go to a place, borrow the people's story, and head off again—is no longer enough. I've started rummaging through old notebooks, re-reading yesterday's stories and discovering the pleasure of returning, of staying, of living each place calmly, thinking only about where I am, finding out what happened to the people I once wrote about and trying to tell the end of their story. What has happened to Vothy? If I really do care—and I've thought of her dozens of times while in other places—I haven't done anything to show it. The years have passed, I've returned to Cambodia, and I haven't visited the Russian hospital. Next time I'm here, I've told myself, next year, tomorrow tomorrow tomorrow . . .

It's raining when we arrive at the Russian hospital. A few patients are lying in the doorway, dying. One dead person leaves, another arrives. We go up to the third floor and meet a nurse in the hallway. She says that she doesn't remember the little girl from the photograph, that she's only been working there a few months. We walk down the hall all the way to the other end and then go back downstairs. The nursery for orphaned children is in a forgotten corner. Tun is sitting cross-legged against the wall reading a story to two little children with AIDS. We sit down beside her; she acknowledges us with a glance and keeps reading. When the story is over, I pull out the photo I took the day I saw Vothy for the last time and show it to her.

"Little Baldy . . ." says Tun, staring at the image.

She's silent a few seconds and leans her head back. Her eyes grow wet, and when she squeezes them shut, a tear slides down her cheek.

"She died," she says, breaking out into disconsolate sobs.

The antiretroviral medicines that were saving AIDS patients on the upper decks of this new *Titanic*, as Dr. Richner had described it, had not reached Cambodia's third-class passengers. No one had done anything to save the patients in the Russian hospital: not the large multinational pharmaceutical companies, not the foreign governments who had done so much to devastate this country, and of course not the local government, whose prime minister lives in the largest mansion in Southeast Asia, protected by tanks. Vothy's medicines could wait.

Tun kept taking little Baldy to Dr. Richner's hospital for several months, standing in line at six in the morning to get the vitamins that kept her immune system alert. Everything was fine until Tun had to go to the countryside for a few weeks to visit her family. Nobody at the hospital bothered to take Vothy to see the Swiss doctor while Tun was gone. The little girl stopped taking her medicines and began to grow weaker, still caring for her mother as she ignored her own illness. By the time Tun returned, it was too late. Vothy was dying of tuberculosis by Sokgan's side. Her tiny body was covered in sores and had deteriorated so much that she had begun to look like her mother. Tun ran down the corridors, shouting at the nurses and berating the only doctor she found on duty.

"You just couldn't take her, could you? You had to let her die like this. You don't care what happens to these people . . ."

It is difficult to believe that Vothy died before her mother did. I had seen the two of them myself, one of them full of life and joy, the other wasting away, trapped between conflicting desires: a yearning to put an end to her own agony and an understandable wish to survive for her daughter's sake. The father, Kong Thai, had stopped bringing mangos to eat and slipping into bed to make love to what was left of his wife. Everyone assumed he was dead and didn't ask about him again. Sokgan no longer harbored any warm feelings for her rickshaw driver, but when he stopped showing up at the hospital, she realized that his disappearance left Vothy a little more alone in the world and made it all the more difficult for her to let herself depart. It was perhaps for that reason that she made a final effort and hung on a few weeks longer.

The light in Vothy's eyes gradually grew dim, and in her last moments she knew more surely than ever that the patients who leave the Russian hospital aren't going anywhere. Her chest became a single black sore; she looked around in terror and found only her mother. Vothy and Sokgan died clutching each other on the rickety bed that had been their home for the last few months, slowly fading away. Like Cambodia, they had never been the masters of their destiny, not until those final moments when Sokgan managed to cling to life a little longer than her daughter and invert the timing of their departure, just as the monsoon reverses the course of the river of evil memory.

Chuan the Invincible

I tell Masa to slow down or she's going to get us killed.

"Don't worry," she says, smiling serenely as she swerves her taxi around fried banana vendors and guns past the motorized trishaws of Bangkok. "If something bad is meant to happen, it will."

"So it doesn't matter if we run all the red lights," I ask. "If our time hasn't arrived, we will never crash?"

"He is taking care of us," she says, pointing at a small figurine of Opasi, the protective monk of the Bangmot temple hanging from the rearview mirror.

A few years ago, Masa had an accident. Her taxi skidded and crashed against a concrete wall in downtown Bangkok. The car was totaled, but she escaped with a few scratches and a broken leg. A few days before the accident, a friend had given her a miniature Opasi.

"He disappeared after the accident. He had fulfilled his mission: to save my life," says Masa, who has upped her protection by adding an extra monk figurine to her dashboard. "Now I bring two monks with me instead of one to make sure at least one is awake while I am driving."

Masa is proud to be known as Thailand's first female taxi driver. She still keeps the yellowed newspaper clippings announcing her appointment with a photograph in which she appears twenty years younger. She didn't choose the job; life did it for her. She needed a new start after fleeing an abusive husband who would beat her for half the week and spend the other half cavorting in the massage parlors of the city's red light districts. There never was a need to hire a private investigator or look for lipstick stains on his shirts.

"I knew he was cheating on me because at night he returned home cleaner than when he had left in the morning," she tells me. "Five minutes after he was back the whole house smelled of salts and aromatic soaps. I wouldn't have cared if he had done it now that I am older, but back then I was still an attractive woman. Why did he have to go with other women?"

Masa left for good. For a while she took any job that was available, working as a waiter or a cleaner. But one day she came across an ad for an unusual job in the local newspaper at a time when women were expected to stay home and wait for the husband to arrive from the massage parlor: "Novotel hotel looking for seven ladies to drive its limousines."

If there was something Masa knew how to do, it was driving. Her father, a police officer, taught her how to drive and outmaneuver the Bangkok *tuk tuk* drivers when she was a little girl. Neighbors turned their heads, scandalized, when they saw a twelve year old behind the steering wheel of the only police car in the district. They couldn't very well file a complaint. After all, sitting in the passenger seat next to Masa was the only policeman in charge of enforcing traffic regulations within a several-mile radius.

Masa was the only female applicant to reply to the Novotel ad. She got the job and has spent most of her waking life behind the wheel ever since. After leaving the Novotel, she worked as a chauffeur for car-rental companies, airport limousine services and, at one time or another, nearly every five-star hotel in the city. One day she decided it was time to become her own boss. Borrowing cash from friends, she bought this second-hand Toyota taxi that is taking us at full speed through the streets of Bangkok. The car seems on the verge of falling apart at any minute. Punished by a life on the potholed Bangkok streets, it has endured countless engine repairs, endless body work, and half a million miles on its weary axles. Or is it a million? The odometer stopped counting long ago.

We pass the neon lights of the red light districts and massage parlors. Like other taxi drivers, Masa keeps brochures from different brothels with photos of the girls so her customers can comparison shop. If taxi drivers steer enough passengers to the brothels, some owners will pay them back in kind: a free night with the girl of their choosing. Masa prefers to take her commission in cash. Even now, years after leaving her husband, it's not easy for her to ask customers if they want to have a good time, say that she knows the best place, clean and well priced, where the owner is discreet and the girls are all university students. Masa sees the contradiction: her husband fell for the same temptation she is now offering to her passengers, whether they are Thai or *farang*, the Thai word for foreigner. But the bigger contradiction she sees is working fourteen hours a day and not making a decent living. So she keeps what seems to her a paradox of life—and the photos of the Bangkok girls—hidden in her glove compartment and brings it out every time she is short of cash.

As we pass the brothels on Soi Cowboy, Masa tells me that, at times, she can't help but feel envious of the young girls at the massage parlors and bars, at least those who have found a good boss who doesn't exploit them or take their money away.

"They earn more in an hour than I do in a whole day," she says.

"And your dignity, Masa?" I ask.

She looks at me as though I've just asked a dumb question. "What's so dignified about spending fourteen-hour days in the middle of Bangkok's traffic or cleaning the bathrooms in the Soi Cowboy bars?"

Over the years, Masa has become a distant relative of sorts that I visit now and again. Whenever I'm in Bangkok on assignment, I give her a call. She picks me up and we head for a street demonstration, a meeting at a government office, or a visit to the slums. I find it admirable that the day she left home and was faced with the only three options that society had reserved for her—another useless husband, the mop and bucket, or a massage parlor—she decided to reject all three, take the driving seat of her life, and break all the taboos of the time by raising her children on her own. I have forgotten where I flagged her taxi down for the first time, but I still remember our first run through the streets of Bangkok. She told me the story of her life in her broken English spiced with humor. I'm picky when it comes to taxi drivers. So when I come across one I like,

I stick with him or her and promise to stay faithful through traffic jams and speeding. Without noticing, mile by mile, some of them have become my friends.

So eight years after that first run, here we are, Masa and I, discussing her retirement plans, the sorry state of men ("they don't want me because I know more about life than they do"), and whether the red light she just ran might hasten our date with destiny. Letting my comment pass, Masa just smiles and looks at her dear monk Opasi out of the corner of her eye.

"Forgive this *farang*," she tells him smiling. "He's not a bad guy, but there are things he will never understand."

We arrive at the Sangmorakot boxing camp early in the afternoon. We have come here often in the last few years. The camp sits just behind the Sitaram Temple in the old part of Bangkok. The owner, Thitiphong Aumanum, rented the land from the monks when he decided to quit his job as a policeman and dedicate himself to training poor boys to become what he had once dreamed about himself: champions of Thai boxing. Sangmorakot is a special place, a strange balance between the peace of the temple and the violence of the fights, meditation and action, boxers' sweat and the neatness of the monks. Once in a while, the monks with their shaved heads and orange robes hang out around the ring and follow the training sessions, discussing amongst themselves whether this or that boxer has a chance of winning his next fight. Monastic life can be a bit tedious at time, and they bet small change on the Saturday fights. Nothing that would awaken greed, of course, just to kill time.

Muay Thai is the national sport of Thailand. It was born within the old Army of Siam as a form of training and preparation to turn soldiers' bodies into weapons. During that era, long before the time when victory in war could be achieved by sending precision missiles from a ship berthed hundreds of miles away or from a combat jet hidden above the clouds, battles were still decided by hand-to-hand combat and soldiers looked each other in the eyes.

They shared the same fear of death.

During their training, Thai troops faced each other without gloves or protective padding. The only rule was, well, that there was none. An official code of conduct was added at the beginning of the twentieth century along with the introduction of gloves and the division of fights into five rounds. Aside from fists, Thai boxers are allowed to strike each other with elbows, knees and feet. The combats are so violent, the contact so brutal, that five rounds are considered just as punishing as ten or twelve rounds of Western boxing. I guess Masa was right when she told me there are two venues where Thais lose their renowned smoothness and politeness: the road and the ring. "We fight well and drive terribly," she says.

The fighters of Sangmorakot are all peasant boys from the poor northern provinces whose families have sent them to the capital to try their luck. It's what Thitiphong, the owner, calls "the Shot." Thitiphong believes everybody deserves one shot—and no more. If you waste that chance, leave your place to the next kid in line and don't come asking for another. The Boss takes any kids who knock on his door asking for that one shot. He feeds them, clothes them, takes them to school, and then trains them so hard they feel pain in muscles they never knew existed. In return, he expects to make some money off them by betting in the fights.

"They are my children," Thitiphong says of his fighters.

For the boys who make it to Sangmorakot—a few of them younger than nine years old—life is confined to the boxing ring. During the day they train, eat, and rest on its canvas-covered floor. When night falls, exhausted and bruised, the child boxers crawl into the space underneath the ring, divided in minute cubbyholes where they huddle together among empty cans and dirty clothes. Those who can't find a spot underneath sleep above, on the canvas, with a net to protect them from mosquitoes. Mosquitoes . . . people from the tropics do not take them lightly. It's difficult to imagine how such a minute and annoying insect has brought nations to their knees, defeated armies and kept entire countries from developing. Mosquitoes kill more people than do hunger, wars, and traffic accidents combined. Even in modern cities such as Bangkok, mosquito-borne diseases such as dengue fever still exist. A boxer with dengue fever is unable to train for weeks; if he hasn't fully recuperated before the day of the fight, then he has very little chance of winning. The fever weakens his body, his muscles hurt, his pulse accelerates, he feels thirsty before the fight, and his body is slow to respond. During the fight, instead of seeing just one opponent, he'll see two. He can't beat both.

The rest of this open-air training camp consists of a rusted scale, a fan, some lumpy boxing bags, and a picture of the abbot of the Sitaram temple. A sign written on the mirror where the boxers practice their moves reminds them of the three basic rules that govern the place:

Work hard.
When you feel exhausted, keep working.
If you think you cannot keep working, continue.

The pictures of past champions who once trained here hang on one wall. They all took their one opportunity and fought all the way to Lumpini Stadium, the arena reserved for the best. The Boss has put the photographs there to remind the young fighters that they too have a chance to cross the fragile bridge of glass that can take them to the other side, where dreams of glory and money await.

Chuan Thummabat is the camp's latest arrival. He is twelve years old, he weighs thirty kilograms (sixty-six pounds), and he has nothing to lose. He has pointy ears and eyes that seem to flash with fear, always alert as if he is expecting something bad to happen to him at any moment. Chuan comes from Korat, the poorest region in the country, a place where the magic of the seasons never seems to work for its people. It is the one dry patch in an otherwise fertile and rich land. Thailand receives from the mountains on its border with Burma all the water it needs to color its northwestern farms every luminous shade of green. The Chao Phraya river, which carves its way south through the country's heart, bathes the lowland rice fields and gives life to its old and new capitals of Ayutthaya and Bangkok respectively. The Andaman Sea and the Gulf of Thailand, with their white sand beaches and emerald waters, attract thousands of tourists and give steady employment to the coastal communities.

But Korat?

The fields of the northeastern plateau, separated from the rest of Thailand by the mountains of Phetchabun, are hard to cultivate. The monsoon arrives there late or early, with too little water or too much. One year brings drought, the next brings floods, and sometimes both hit in the same season. For the inhabitants of Korat, the only sure path to success leads in one direction: out. The young people do not want to inherit the lives of their parents and grandparents, always at the mercy of the seasons. So they leave for the capital with the hope that they will never return. The measure of success is that simple: if you return home, you have failed. But to have any chance of becoming a champion of Muay Thai, you have to start very young and become a man before you are even close to being one.

Turning children into men is the Boss's main task.

Chuan made the journey to the city by bus, crossing the country with just a bag that held a change of clothes, something to eat, and a few coins. The previous year's drought had convinced his parents that there was no future for the boy in Korat. Why not try their luck with Chuan? If he became a champion the family would never have to struggle again; no one would care about the monsoon being a month or even a year late. Let it not come at all, if it didn't want to.

"Do what your master says and you'll be a champion," Chuan's father said to the boy on the day of his departure.

Chuan was dropped off at the Sitaram temple doors and that same day he got his head shaved. After being introduced to the other kids, he was issued a T-shirt, a pair of shorts, and his first pair of boxing gloves. He was told: train hard and you will become a champion. He was told: everybody has a task, and the newest arrival – you – must clean the toilets. He was told: Sangmorakot is a family where your triumphs are secondary to the camp's, the group is more important than the individual. He was told: obey the rules or else you will be sent back to the barren fields of Korat.

"What is your fighter's nickname?" a trainer asked him.

"I don't have one," Chuan replied.

"Well, from now on you will be . . . the Invincible. The Invincible One of Sangmorakot."

Life hasn't changed much for Chuan. He used to wake up at 5 a.m. to work in the fields with his father. He does it now to train. At Sangmorakat, the day begins with an eight-kilometer (five-mile) run around the temple. This is followed by a session of jumping rope, lifting weights, and a full hour of throwing legs, elbows, and fists at the old punching bag hanging from the ceiling. And then, hardest of all for little guys like Chuan, the two hundred push-ups.

"One, two, three, four . . . !" shouts the Boss, his mobile phone always ready to organize the next fight with rival promoters. "I don't want those noses touching the ground. Keep going. Five, six, seven, eight . . . !"

After the early-morning training, Chuan takes his knapsack and heads to a nearby school. Classes finish by 3 p.m., and Chuan goes back to Sangmorakat for more training until dark. Thin as a stick, he spends hours in hand-to-hand combat with other children, sometimes the bigger ones. Knocked to the floor over and over, he keeps struggling to get back up on his feet to face his next opponent. A punch in the face, a kick in his belly, a knee thrust in the side . . . After dinner, sore and exhausted, Chuan crawls under the ring and finds a place to sleep.

Work hard.
When you feel exhausted, keep working.
If you think you cannot keep working, continue.

Chuan's first fights have not gone well. In the last bout, his face was badly cut, but the referee refused to stop the fight. When the canvas got too splattered with blood, the referee simply separated the boxers for a few minutes and ordered a ringside attendant to douse the ring with a bucket of water. A trainer put a bandage on the cuts above Chuan's eyes, and he trudged out to endure two more rounds. The wounds have now earned him three days of rest. There will be no training until the swelling subsides and he can see clearly with both eyes. It's a welcome respite from the training, but he knows he must improve if he wants to stay. So far, his record is not encouraging: seven fights, seven losses.

It's always the same up in the ring. From the opening bell, the Invincible One is paralyzed, his mind blocked. He can't remember the kicks and punches he learned at the camp, nor can he summon up the hunger for victory that consumes most migrants from Korat. Fear takes over. He covers his face with his fists to avoid the blows or lowers them to protect his stomach, but he seems unable to strike back. Of the twenty boys at Sangmorakot, he is the only one who has failed to notch a single victory. Where is he hiding the fury that fires up the other boys, the determination to do whatever to catch the Shot? Muay Thai champions have to harden themselves in local amateur fights. Each victory raises their cachet; each defeat lowers their chances of ever fighting again. If the boxer loses, no one will want to bet on him, he won't appear on the posters, and he'll be sent home. Most of the boys at Sangmorakot await the next chance to fight like Western children anticipate the arrival of Santa Claus. It can never come soon enough, that moment when they can shorten the distance to the other side of the bridge of dreams. But Chuan only longs to postpone the arrival of the next fight. He wishes it would never come.

Thitiphong arrives at the camp, bringing a poster announcing the next boxing night he has organized with another promoter in the city of Ratchaburi, at the local Sing Yu Stadium. A full slate of betting fights has been organized, and everybody but Chuan strains to see their names on the poster. The Boss announces the matches one by one, leaving Chuan's until the end: "In the thirty-kilogram category: the Invincible One of Sangmorakot against the Tiger of Supanburi," he says, before turning to the kids. "The fight is in eight days. Everybody back to work."

Ratchaburi is an hour and a half drive from Bangkok in the direction of Hua Hin, the vacation spot of the Thai royal family. Chuan has arrived a day early, so he can be rested before tonight's fight. He's woken up early in the morning and before breakfast he accompanies his opponent to the stadium for the weigh-in. The old scales at the camp can't be trusted, so this moment is decisive. If the Invincible One of Sangmorakot weighs just one pound more than the stipulated weight, he'll only have a few hours to lose it or he'll be disqualified. The last time this happened, the Boss wouldn't let him eat anything during the day, made him exercise for hours, and forced him to put on warm clothes in the stifling tropical heat so that he would sweat off the extra weight, drop by drop. When Chuan climbed into the ring he was so tired and hungry that he could hardly stand up. That day he suffered the worst beating of his life.

The two boys strip and step up onto the scales:

Chuan the Invincible—sixty-six pounds.
The Supanburi Tiger—sixty-six pounds.

Chuan knows what it means to get his weight right: rice, meat, and chicken soup: the fight-day feast. The purse for the fight has been set at nearly eight dollars for each boy and a few more for the winner. A win that gives bettors a good sum will guarantee an extra portion of the purse for the boxers, but no one wants to bet their money on someone who has lost every fight. The bets are ten to one against the Invincible. If he loses again, he'll be sent home.

Sing Yu Stadium is located on a small side street in the city of Ratchaburi. A man without legs begs for a few coins at the entrance. Food stands flavor the air with the smell of Thai spices. Photographs of King Bhumibol hang over the ring. The monarch has reigned over twenty-two different governments, lived through eighteen coups d'état and stayed six decades on the throne to become the closest Thais have to a deity. His endurance alone qualifies him as the greatest fighter of all in the eyes of his people. The traffic in Bangkok still comes to a standstill whenever the Lord of Life leaves the palace: the police close off all bridges to prevent people from looking down on the king when his retinue travels underneath. His image can be seen on buildings, in villages, homes and streets, on necklaces worn by the scantily clad girls who pole-dance in the red light districts, and next to the rock star posters in the bedrooms of adolescents across the country. When you go to the movie theatre in Bangkok, you have to rise in honor of the king before the film begins. If it rains, the Thai government asks the king for advice on what to do. If it rains too much, they ask him how to stop it. In September 2006, I landed in Bangkok on the same day that the army initiated a coup against Prime Minister Thaksin Shinawatra, who had dared to overshadow Bhumibol and the long-standing Thai elite with his accumulation of wealth and power. I took a taxi and headed for the Government House along with Time magazine correspondent Hannah Beech. Smiling soldiers politely apologized to the tourists "for the inconvenience" as they stormed the center of the city. One couldn't help but notice the ribbons that decorated their tanks.

They were yellow as the Sun, the color of King Bhumibol.

A hundred plastic chairs have been added to the stands for the event tonight—an event that is officially illegal. The government prohibits fights with boxers under fifteen or those whose weight is less than forty-five kilograms. The brains of the children are not completely formed and the constant blows in the head delay their mental development, in some cases forever. At a nearby hospital, one of the doctors wearily tells me that his shifts last longer on fighting days: "On occasion they bring boys with serious injuries, but we usually just have to stitch them up here and there and in a few days they're back in the ring." The betting mafias have a different interpretation of the law: the lighter the boxer, the greater the amount of money betted against his improbable victory and the fatter the profits if he takes a surprise win. The fights are organized now outside Bangkok, in places like Ratchaburi, to avoid the police. The Boss could make good money tonight if Chuan wins.

Thitiphong gives his last instructions for the fight, repeating his old theory that boxing is like any other job. A boxer needs to think as much as a surgeon or a lawyer. If the surgeon does not think, he loses his patient in the operating room. If the lawyer does not think, his client goes to jail. If the boxer does not think, he will get hurt.

"How can you expect to win if you receive enough blows to make you dimmer than you already are?" the Boss asks. "The three weapons of Muay Thai, my boy, are body, heart, and mind. Leave one at home and you will be sorry. Understood?"

"I understand," replies Chuan, his voice trembling and inaudible.

"Body, Heart, and Mind. What are you going to do during the fight?

"I will use my head, Boss."

"Well, that's my boy."

The first fight of the evening is in the fifty-two-pound category: Sivagon versus Denphimaai. Neither has turned eight and their boxing gear, their gloves and shorts, look like a costume from a school dress-up party. But the bell rings and their child's innocence transforms into fury. It's not your typical schoolyard fight where the participants shove and hit each other randomly; the boys' movements are coordinated, their punches precise and hard. They take their opponent's blows without complaining, and when they're knocked down they spring to their feet again. When the round is over, the bell sounds and they don't dare to move, waiting for their trainers to lift them by their arms and take them to their respective corners. A bit of water, ice for their legs, a couple of slaps, and it's back to the ring. At the end of the fight, the judges give their notes to the referee and Sivagon is declared winner of the match. His trainers pull him into their arms and embrace him; he is then set down on his stool in the corner of the ring where he is given his share of the purse. Unable to grasp the money with his gloved hands, he opens his mouth and someone places the bills between his teeth. He bites down hard on the cash. The money's his and no one can take it from him. He's earned it.

Thailand finds itself halfway between the First and Third Worlds. If we imagine a one-thousand-mile highway between them—often just a dirt road—the country has probably reached the five-hundred-mile marker. In such a place, the poor are an embarrassing and constant reminder of what the country wished had been left behind for good. But there they are, the poor, still showing in the rear-view mirror of the car every time you look back during the long and tortuous journey. I remember when Thai leaders decided to clean up Bangkok days before the 2003 Asia-Pacific Economic Cooperation (APEC) summit, one of the many useless meetings that are held to justify politicians' salaries and which journalists insist on attending just to waste time. The government decided that their guests could not see that reflection in the mirror—poverty—when they crossed the city in their BMWs. Nearly ten thousand homeless people were removed from the streets and taken to military camps, Hercules-130 aircraft were used to move Cambodian beggars out of the country, and the largest slum area of the city was covered by an enormous four-story, five-hundred-yard billboard that featured a picture of the Royal Palace. That illusory facade, conveniently placed so as to conceal from the world the reality that lay beyond it, a reality the slum residents were painfully aware of, could have been easily set on fire by slum residents in protest. I don't think it was their respectful reverence towards the king that prevented them from doing so. The slum residents had become so accustomed to being ignored that they assumed it was expected of them to remain invisible.

Thai boxing is, as in the case of soccer in Brazil or cricket in India, one of the few opportunities available to those who aspire to complete the passage to visibility. A few years ago I met Parinya Charoenphol, one of the greatest national boxing champions whose life story was brought to film by local director Ekachai Uekrongtham. Ever since he was a child, Parinya's dream was to become a woman. For years he boxed as a man in order to achieve his dream of becoming that woman. He used the money earned with each victory to make his transformation more evident. His gestures became increasingly feminine, he began to wear makeup and his femininity made his wins all the more humiliating for his opponents. With each victory the transformation accelerated: longer hair, tighter shorts, a bra, perfume, and finally his refusal to undress for the traditional contenders' weigh-in ceremony before the fight.

"When I finally earned enough money for the sex change operation, boxing didn't make sense anymore. I achieved my dream," he explained.

The child boxers at Sangmorakot camp have simpler dreams. A house for their parents, a better life, or to never be looked down upon in this country wrought with marked social differences. To belong. With its intermittent democracy and deficiencies, Thailand has managed to break through the lethargy of poverty and give its citizens opportunities. Yet for many, becoming a boxing champion is the only way to become part of the elite. Or, rather, to just barely escape from the lowest class; because the elite will invite you to their houses on occasion if you finally make it and fight at Lumpini Stadium. They'll exhibit you to their friends in much the same way someone shows off a mascot, but they'll never accept you as one of them. You won't be invited to their daughters' weddings and you can rest assured that you won't be marrying one of them. So when you ask the boys of Sangmorakot about their dreams, they'll always start talking about fame and money, a sports car and a house, but as they continue talking about what they really want and what their aspirations are, they reveal what it is they're really fighting for each time they jump into the ring.

They want others to notice them—to become visible.

The Invincible One of Sangmorakot awaits his turn to enter the ring in a corner of the Sing Yu stadium. Today more than ever he has that look in his eyes I noticed when we first met, always alert, in constant fear. His opponent is next to him, jumping up and down and throwing punches in the air. The Tiger of Supanburi has participated in eight fights. He has won all of them. The trainers begin to prepare the little boxers for combat. They bandage the kids' knuckles, grease their bodies in oil, smear their faces with petroleum jelly and massage their muscles, all the while reminding them of their strategies.

"What are you going to do during the fight?"

"I am going to use my head."

By tradition, boxers must climb into the ring surpassing the highest rope, symbolizing that God is above all things. Neither Chuan nor his rival is tall enough to reach the last cord, so they squish underneath like two squirrels. They start dancing the traditional Wai Kru, moving like warriors in honor of their masters and kneeling down to pray to Buddha in each of the four corners. The ring has been sealed against bad spirits. The referee approaches the boxers, checks their genitals to verify that they are wearing the protective cup, and gives the green light.

The sound of the bell announces the first of five rounds. Both boxers move from side to side, studying each other's movements. The Tiger attacks first, advancing towards the Invincible One and delivering a lightning-fast kick to his face. Chuan staggers. Then comes a punch to his face, another kick, a knee to the stomach.

"Move, Chuan, why aren't you moving?" his coach asks from the corner.

The Invincible One retreats a step and the Tiger follows him until he has Chuan cornered against the ropes. He grabs Chuan's neck with both hands and begins to knee him repeatedly in the stomach. The crowd cheers each blow and begins hurling taunts at the Invincible One: "Go away, kid!" "What are you doing here?" "A baby would fight better."

"Move, move, MOVE!" the coaches' screams get louder.

Chuan feels the pain. The pain from each blow. The pain from the cheers and the laughs coming from the crowd. The pain from just being here. He desperately seeks help, looking everywhere, but finds none. The faces around tell him: you are alone, nobody can help you now. They tell him: one shot, that's all you get. They tell him: you are not made for boxing, boy, go back to the barren fields of Korat.

"Has anybody checked this guy's record?" asks Chuan's coach from the corner. "Eight fights, eight victories. He is going to kill our boy."

The blows hit Chuan incessantly. The Invincible One kneels down and raises a fist requesting a stop to everything, the fragile crystal bridge of dreams breaking under his feet long before he has reached the other side. The referee begins the countdown.

"One, two . . . can you keep on?"

Silence.

"Three, four . . . can you keep on?"

Silence.

Is it the fear of losing that paralyzes him or the fear of winning? Perhaps it would be better to just give up. Why not give away the opportunity he never wanted and return home to wait for the rain, back to a life of yearning for the change of seasons, you Child of the Monsoon?

"Five, six, seven, eight . . . "

Chuan stands up in the middle of the ring and looks from side to side, with that frightened look on his face. Eight fights, eight defeats.

It is all over and he can leave, but he can't. He is standing, immobile, in the middle of the ring, still paralyzed by fear. His right brow has swollen up and his left cheekbone is bruised. The coach comes into the ring, picks Chuan up and carries him over his shoulder. The Boss seems to want to say something to him, to try to cheer him up perhaps, but he says nothing. On their return to Bangkok that night, the Sangmorakot team sits in silence after one victory and two defeats. The Invincible One arrives at the camp in the early hours of the morning. He looks for a spot to sleep and lies down among the rest of the boys.

Another boy, still awake, approaches Chuan. "How was the fight, Invincible?"

"I lost."

Masa couldn't come along to see Chuan's fight at Ratchaburi. Things aren't going very well for her at home. Her daughter is going through a separation; it seems her husband also came home cleaner than when he left in the morning—the house also smelled of scented salts. Masa now lives in a tiny house on the outskirts of Bangkok with her daughter, her granddaughter and her son, who has just turned twenty. Masa was newly separated and pregnant with her first-born when she began to work as a taxi driver. She spent most of her pregnancy behind the wheel. Her customers couldn't believe what they were seeing: a lady taxi driver in the then yet-to-be modernized Bangkok, and about to give birth. Masa travelled so many miles in her taxi during her nine-month pregnancy that when the child was born, she couldn't think of a better name for her son: Miles.

"I worry about Miles," she says as we race through the city. "The boy gets into fights. The other day a gang attacked him and took his cell phone. I'm afraid that they're going to hurt him. I want to send him to a monastery, to become a monk. I have to speak to the abbot of a temple near my house, so that they can take him in for a few months. Maybe he'll calm down while he's there."

I tell Masa that I'm not sure that the temple is the solution to Miles' problems. I think she is again glancing at Opasi.

"Forgive this *farang*, there are some things he will never understand."

Masa believes that Buddhism will save Miles in the same way it saved her in that accident in downtown Bangkok. She thinks that the problem with today's youth is that they want everything and they don't settle for just anything, that they long for today—don't mention tomorrow, tomorrow's too late. In the eyes of Buddhism, they are incapable of controlling their material ambitions, and therefore, they've lost their freedom. Buddha didn't promise his followers salvation on Earth, only the end of their suffering if they managed to control their earthly desires. But younger generations don't seem to be able to control them as well as their parents did. The country has progressed rapidly in recent years; yet its peoples' expectations have done it even faster.

Masa has witnessed all the changes of the last two decades from the driver's seat of her taxi. She's seen the shopping malls popping up over the rice fields, her neighbors changing the way they dress and those traditional markets replaced by fashionable restaurants and nightclub terraces. And she's seen it all as though it was a wheel of life, unavoidable and unstoppable. When Masa drives through the streets of Bangkok at top speed, she doesn't believe that our fate will be determined by her competence or how safe a driver she is, because everything has been written for us. Perhaps the next intersection will be her last, her ticket to her next, better life, and if it is to be, then there's nothing she can do to alter destiny. The belief that everything is pre-ordained is not necessarily a bad way of facing those long days behind the wheel in one of the worst cities in the world to be a taxi driver. The pay is terrible, competition nasty, and the traffic jams nothing less than infernal. In recent years, the government has invested in above-ground rail and subway systems, but many people still take their car. Some do so because public transportation lines don't reach their homes. Others simply won't—they have waited twenty years to be able to afford a car. Now that they finally have one, they will drive it through hell if necessary.

"Traffic is impossible," Masa says. Yet here she is again, enjoying this latest traffic jam that has trapped the both of us, almost savoring it—because it could be her last. She still has the energy to keep on and her old Toyota has some years left in it. But the law says otherwise.

According to the regulations, a taxi must be taken out of circulation after twelve years of service. The last second-hand taxi Masa bought was six years old. Year after year, she's dutifully paid back the debt she incurred on the car, the license, repairs, and the bodywork needed after those "small accidents" that Opasi has always managed to save her from. Now that she's begun to see herself clear of all her debts, to start earning money for herself, and to truly become her own boss, the authorities say that her taxi has to be taken off the road. The regulations are good for the large taxi companies that get rid of their old vehicles by selling them second-hand, buying new ones, and renting them to people like Masa who could never purchase one on their own. The owner of the taxi company, a rich man who is driven through the streets of Bangkok in a limousine, earns vast sums of money by just sitting in his office or playing golf while the poor from the rural areas fill his coffers, thanks to the contracts given to him by his friends in the government.

"They don't make laws for the little people like me. They don't want old cars with no air conditioning on the street," explains Masa, "but it's not fair. I've worked hard for this taxi and just when I'm about to call it my own they tell me I have to buy another one. With what money?"

"What are you going to do?" I ask.

"I'm too old to work at a massage parlor, aren't I?" she laughs. "I need money, so I guess I have to work at a hotel again and put up with a boss telling me what to do."

I too savor that last traffic jam alongside Masa, crossing through neon-lit streets, all the while thinking that life will never be hard enough to knock down my Bangkok taxi driver. I tell Masa that her resilience against all adds is proof enough that nothing is destined, not even what lies beyond the red light we are about to run. If it were all written, Masa, you'd still be sharing your roof with a husband who didn't deserve you, not drawing out the final miles on a taxi that perhaps you never fully owned, but which has nevertheless put you in the driver's seat of your own life.

Reneboy

The train that passes through the San Antonio slum is always late and unreliable; it never announces its arrival, never stops. When its dark shape appears in the distance, someone yells "Traaaaaaaain!" and the women stop pressing against the rails, the men gulp down the last of their drinks, and the children playing on the tracks get out of the way. Every now and then someone—young or old, or maybe just drunk—doesn't manage to get out of the way in time, and people have to search for the body parts, piece them back together like a jigsaw puzzle, and place them in an old wooden box for the funeral. Everyone has a friend or relative who took the train to nowhere. Jose was hit when he was buying cigarettes at one of the stalls by the tracks; little Raymond, six years old, chased a basketball in front of the train; and old Marco was cut in two when he fell asleep outside the door of his house with his legs extended.

That's life in San Antonio: you live and die on the tracks.

Is it the train that slices through the slum, or the slum that impedes the train's passage? Its residents and the municipal authorities can't seem to come to an agreement on that question.

Not far from San Antonio, in the financial district of Makati, there's a place named for money. Forbes, it's called. Its residents live in fortified opulence, shielded from the poverty around it by six-meter walls topped with barbed wire and security guards armed with rifles. The residents of Forbes have no idea that in Manila the garbage goes uncollected for weeks: they have their own pickup service with prompt, silent trucks, their streets as clean as Melbourne's, with sidewalks that meander among green lawns large enough for a round of golf. The residents of Forbes are also oblivious to the pathetic state of local public health facilities because the men get their cysts removed in Hong Kong and their wives get their skin stretched in Bangkok. In Forbes, some people don't even know how bad the traffic's been of late. The richest of the rich—the ones with the biggest mansions and the numbest consciences—get around by helicopter, touching down on the rooftops of buildings that, if they aren't theirs already, will be soon enough. They hover above everything, untainted by the human jungle and the chaos below them.

This is Manila: a brutal mixture of San Antonio and Forbes.

Breaking news comes in over the wire at the *El Mundo* bureau in Hong Kong. It says, "Avalanche of garbage kills more than two hundred in Philippines." The teletype offers a bit more: the government is blaming the monsoon rains for the tragedy, claiming that they weakened the base of a trash heap thirty meters tall in the district of Payatas, where more than eighty thousand people live around the country's largest landfill. The problem, it seems, is not that all those people were living next to piles of trash because they had no other place to go. It has simply rained too much. Witnesses recount how they heard a loud rumble in the middle of the night, and when they went out to see what was happening, they saw that the great mountain had collapsed. The three hundred shanties at its base had disappeared under an avalanche of waste. The cries of the people trapped beneath the trash grew gradually quiet, one by one, until by dawn they could no longer be heard. Parents tried to get to their children, children searched for their mothers, but a wall of impassable garbage stood between them and their loved ones.

The site of the tragedy is known as Lupang Pangako, the Promised Land. Are all those people in the landfill's way, or has the landfill invaded their space? Authorities and residents have been unable to come to an agreement on this either.

In the early '70s, Payatas was sufficiently invisible and remote that the country's elite wouldn't have acknowledged its existence. The government decided to use it as the city's trash can, setting aside 23.3 hectares of land as a dumping zone. With Manila's rapid growth, city authorities were "forced" to displace the people living in the shantytowns to make way for new shopping centers, apartment buildings, and highways. They solved the problem by sending them to a place where they wouldn't bother anyone. Payatas gradually filled up with the homeless, the desperate, and the forsaken. A piece of ownerless land is an extraordinary thing in this country, where a few hundred families control half the land, two-thirds of the wealth, and all the political power to make sure nothing changes. A piece of land, even in the middle of unspeakable squalor, is Promised Land.

In the Hong Kong airport, on my way to Manila to cover the story, I've called Raymond. The child of another Manila slum, Raymond is slight, with a voice that's perpetually hoarse. He has learned enough English to get a job as an errand boy in the offices of the Singaporean newspaper, *The Straits Times.* When I come to Manila, I hire him as an interpreter. He puts the money he earns in the piggybank where he keeps all his savings for what he says will be the business of his life: he plans to buy a number of secondhand computers and install a videogame parlor in the living room of his house, which is strategically located across from a school. He's full of dreams; his wife just fumes.

"What did you expect?" I ask Raymond. "I'm surprised she let you back in the house after proposing something like that."

"But it can't fail," he explains, laying out the details of expenses and revenues. "I'll earn enough to give our son an education and my wife can buy all the dresses she wants. We'll have to get used to having a lot of kids in the house, but the business is a sure thing."

We rent a car and drive to the Promised Land. No directions are necessary. Before we even arrive, a powerful odor of rotten fish seeps in through the car windows. It's so strong that we can barely detect the one we expected, of hundreds of corpses still buried under the garbage. The smell pierces your nostrils, burrows inside you, jangles your senses, and clings to your brain for hours, even days, after you've left it. It's not really an odor, but a mixture of all the worst possible odors, which together form a single, unbearable stench.

It's the stench of poverty.

Hardly twenty-four hours have passed since the collapse, and the residents of Payatas have gone back to work, the fates of their friends, neighbors, and family members still uncertain. The hum of activity in the dump is evidence not of indifference toward the dead but of the desperate straits of the living. When you get by on a dollar a day, you're not going to give up that dollar for anything; you have to do what it takes to get it or you won't be able to eat. Or, worse, your children won't be able to eat. The dead no longer need their dollar; the people they left behind still do.

The Promised Land doesn't look like any other place on earth that I've seen, not even the other landfills inhabited by the desperately poor. It is, quite literally, a city of garbage. The shanties, built from cast-off materials, squat on the slopes of enormous mounds of refuse that grow ever taller with additional cans, bottles, tires, plastic, used shavers, out-of-date magazines, old black-and-white televisions—who wants a black-and-white TV these days?—rusted washing machines, and thousands of other items that have served out their purpose in the big city and been replaced by others, which themselves, sooner or later, will end up here. The piles of debris form small vales, cliffs, mountains, and alleyways. There's a school in one corner and, further along, a basketball court, a church, a fish market swarming with flies. People who have the space for a couple of chickens have built fences from mattress springs, while others have cut curtains for their huts from the remnants of old dresses. The children roll down the streets on scooters made from trashcan lids and shopping cart wheels. Nothing is left over in this city of what's left over.

We've brought masks to protect ourselves from germs and diseases. Or maybe just to protect ourselves from poverty. The government officials and a handful of journalists who've arrived ahead of us are wearing them, too. Raymond thinks we should leave ours in the car.

"Imagine you invite me to dinner at your house and I show up in a HAZMAT suit, like those men in that Spielberg movie when they come to take E.T. away. These people live here every day. We're in their home, even if it looks like a cesspit to us."

We leave the masks behind.

Rising in front of us, a massive mountain of garbage. We head uphill, sinking a little deeper into the noisome mire with each step. Only from the crest of Mount Rubbish, gazing at the horizon from on high, is it possible to understand the meaning of a place like the Promised Land. In the distance, on clear days, you can make out the big city. It doesn't look so far away, and yet for the people rummaging through the trash around us, barefoot and smeared with mud, it is Mars, a remote planet whose existence they hardly recognize. Their only link with that distant world is the dirt road on which the trucks arrive, in a perfect line, like a charging armored division, loaded with more and more scraps in an endless procession. When a truck reaches its destination, the driver turns on the hydraulics and the load container begins to tilt. Hundreds of people follow it with their gaze, first stretching their necks upward and then, when the load begins sliding down the metal, following the garbage until it hits the ground. The container bangs up and down a few times and releases the last bits of debris, and everyone knows the time has come. The garbage is theirs.

A little boy with brown skin, unevenly cropped hair, bruised feet, and protruding ears is rummaging through the trash. He's wearing a grimy white shirt and shorts. He has no shoes. In one hand, he's holding a metal hook, which he uses to clear a path through the trash like a jungle guide. In the other is a bag that he's filling with the little treasures he finds on the way: the head of a broken doll, a scrap of metal, an empty Coca-Cola bottle, an old newspaper with an article on the latest government progress in the fight against poverty . . . Every time a truck arrives, he tries to poke his head into the crowd of desperate people, but they keep pushing him away. He sits down and waits for the others to finish, and then searches through the scraps of the scraps. I ask him his name.

"Reneboy," he says, "son of Fe and Edelberto."

Reneboy is ten years old (he looks seven) and the eighth of ten siblings. Ten children would have been too many in practically any other place on earth, but not in the Philippines in the early 2000s, when Cardinal Sin and President Joseph Estrada hold sway. The former has spent decades battling against any loosening of the restrictions on birth control here, where four thousand babies are born a day, half of whom go straight to the poverty rolls. Recently, when the latter was asked about his failure to limit the country's population, he answered that he comes from a large family and never would have been born had birth control been permitted. What Estrada fails to mention is that Filipinos would have then been spared a corrupt, womanizing drunk for a leader. President Ten Percent, as he's known—no government contract is signed without his taking a cut—meets with his ministers in what's called the "midnight cabinet," which holds long binges that last into the wee hours of morning. His advisor, Aprodicio Laquian, once justified the importance of his own post by noting that he was the only member of the government who was sober when matters of state were discussed.

So Reneboy gets up every day at the same time his president goes to bed—around four in the morning. He picks up his hook and his bag and heads out to gather trash until it's completely full. He knows his mother will be waiting for him at the end of every day with the same question as always.

"Did you fill your bag, Reneboy?"

And if it isn't full, she sends him back out to the mountain to look for a little more nothing. He can only return home to ask for his one daily meal when he's finished his work. Reneboy's stomach has never been full. A little rice here, maybe a little chicken at Christmas, but nothing even close to that sensation when you say, "I can't eat another bite." He sits down on the floor and accepts what he's given. He doesn't complain; he looks at his sister's plate and then turns to his mother as if asking forgiveness, since there's not enough for her, either. "Mom," he says, looking for Fe's approval, "tomorrow I'm going to work really hard." "Yes, Reneboy, tomorrow . . . "

Fe and Edelberto Chale arrived in the Promised Land in 1995, leaving behind a money-losing fruit stand in Talayan on Mindanao Island, where the Muslims have been fighting to establish an Islamic state ever since the Spanish landed on their shores and imposed a new God in the sixteenth century. Edelberto took off for Manila to escape from poverty. His suitcase held little more than a dream that he thought was well within reach, certainly not asking too much: a plot of land, a house, and a job to feed his family. Instead, the city has given him a piece of landfill, a shack, and a position as a garbage-picker. He wonders if it wouldn't have been better to stay where he was. How long can a dream stay alive when it goes unfulfilled? A year? Two? A whole lifetime, maybe? Edelberto kept his alive for a while, but soon the plot of land, the house, and the job stopped showing up in his fantasies. He gave up his life's dream and focused on making the most of his life in the Promised Land.

The place had become the only way out for those who, like him, had nowhere else to go, those who had lost their homes in typhoons or been displaced by urban development, or rural people in flight from a feudal system, passed down through the generations since colonial times, that turned them into the landowners' slaves and left their children without opportunities. Manila's story is the story of São Paulo, Johannesburg, and Jakarta. These cities have been slowly colonized by the poor and desperate, first on the outskirts, where they don't bother anyone, and then, little by little, flooding the city centers, becoming more and more visible, until they create cities within cities, enclaves outside the system's reach.

The countryside has been forsaken by governments around the world: it's a way of life in decline, and nobody wants to live in a place that's been left to its own devices. Instead, they flock to places where great hopes dwell. You have to seek out the neon lights and the wide boulevards, not so much for yourself but to make room for the small possibility that the next generation—your children, perhaps your grandchildren—will have their opportunity. You have to make it to the city, whatever the cost.

Thousands of Edelbertos arrive in Manila on trains that pass through squalid slums like San Antonio and watch their dreams evaporate before they even reach their destination. The city, the myth that persuaded you to leave everything behind, doesn't want you, and now it's too late. You bought a one-way ticket, betting it all on no way back.

The sun has not yet risen, but it's already morning in the Promised Land. Reneboy has assured Fe he'll work hard today. He walks down the main street of the garbage city wearing the same clothes he wore to bed, and other children emerge from their huts, joining the daily march that carries them to the foot of Mount Rubbish. "Reneboy, I'll race you to the top," says Evelyn, a little girl about his size who has her hair pulled back and is wearing clean clothes, as if she were going to a party at school. Everyone starts running uphill.

At the top, Reneboy scans the horizon and says, pointing to the collapsed mountain, "My father says there are thousands of dead people in there."

"Will the worms eat them?" asks Ronald, one of the older boys.

"No, the diggers will get them out," says Reneboy, pointing to the rescue teams that will soon abandon the place without giving them a proper burial.

A brief silence precedes the beginning of the workday. The children start moving like rats through the trash, prodding it with their hooks from time to time, tossing aside any useless items and putting the ones they can sell into their bags. Reneboy hardly lifts his head, scrutinizing the ground until someone announces the arrival of the first truck of the morning. "Run! Hurry!" someone shouts, alerting the others. Many of the older trashpickers are still sleeping, so there's not as much competition. There's no pushing, and the children start swapping their finds—I'll give you this bottle for your piece of plastic, this scrap of cloth for that cardboard box, this sole of a shoe for those two tin cans. The process ensures that each one ends up with the scraps most interesting to the buyer, who will inspect the merchandise to see what can be recycled. The trucks keep coming, and with them a number of beggars. By midmorning, under a relentless tropical sun, the peak of Mount Rubbish has been leveled, and things become much more difficult. There's hardly anything of value left, and the day drags on until near dusk, when Reneboy finally feels like he's collected enough.

Worn out, his feet bare and his legs bruised, Reneboy enters the little shack that Edelberto built from a few pieces of plywood. "Is this enough?" he asks, holding out his bag and displaying the day's treasures. His mother nods and he looks for a space on the floor among his parents and siblings, sinking down exhausted to sleep. His youngest brother, a baby only a few months old, is tucked away in a wicker basket that dangles above the floor so the rats can't bite him. Reneboy recites the Paternoster and closes his eyes. But he's never gotten to sleep until he's had enough and awakened naturally with the rising sun. The trucks return in the middle of the night with Manila's last, best scraps. The rumble of their motors echoes through the family hut near the western slope of Mount Rubbish, announcing the arrival of more trash. And it is then, in the dark of early morning, that the Promised Land actually lives up to its name. The trashpickers carry flashlights so they can see in the darkness; dozens of points of light move back and forth like fireflies, turning the universe of garbage into a constellation of stars. At dawn, everything will be privation once more, but for a few hours, Edelberto and Fe feel like they're in another place.

"Sometimes when I get up in the middle of the night," Fe tells me, "I even think this place is beautiful."

Reneboy says that in his dreams he sees himself driving one of those trash-laden trucks, crossing the Promised Land behind the wheel and honking his horn so they all know he's arrived with more for everyone. In his dreams, he never leaves this place—why would he? This is where he's grown up and this is the only life he knows. The stench of garbage, which the monsoon rains have made intolerable even for the most veteran residents of the Promised Land, is now normal to him. He remembers that once his father took him to the big city, downtown, but he didn't like it. Nobody knows each other, nobody stops to greet each other, nobody looks at anybody else. It's hard to believe: it's easier to find happy people in the Promised Land than in many of the financial centers and wealthy areas on earth. Nobody feels alone here, doors are always open to neighbors, one person's problems are everybody's problems: the place glows with the communal warmth of Filipino slums. Even if your children get sick, even if adult life expectancy is only forty-five years, even if you have to sleep with rats for most of your life, it only takes a few months living in the landfill to forget that things could be different. Life in the Promised Land is survival. Because people's ambitions have adapted to that reality, happiness is more within reach. It does not consist of the latest sports car or a house with a swimming pool; the quest for it does not involve eyeing what anyone else has acquired. Nor is it a goal that, once reached, is easily swapped out for another, one more stop on the endless road to dissatisfaction that they've started down there, on that other planet, in the big city. Happiness in the Promised Land is a plate of warm food, a healthy child, two neighbors chatting at twilight. You can almost touch it.

No, in Reneboy's dreams there is no better life. The piece of land, the house, and the job that drew his father away from his native Mindanao do not exist. Perhaps in time the boy will inherit Edelberto's dreams and they will carry him elsewhere, far from here. Until then, though, Reneboy dreams of a whole series of improbable and fascinating finds in the landfill: sneakers, a remote-controlled car, or food, especially food. Every once in a while, the residents of the Promised Land find the corpse of a gangster shot full of bullets in Tondo to settle a score; the remains of a young woman, raped and abandoned, which they must approach, even touch, to make sure it's not a broken mannequin from one of the shopping centers in Makati; or the aborted fetuses of Malate prostitutes and rich men's daughters, fetuses that here, in the Promised Land, now belong to no class. Nobody talks about any of these finds. Everybody likes talking about the valuable things hidden in the mountains of trash.

"Once I found a gold necklace," Reneboy recalls, his eyes alight as if he were reliving the moment of discovery. "It got tangled on my hook and I ran off so nobody would see it and take it from me. I took it to a pawnshop. I'd never seen so much money at one time. My father and I went to buy as much cement as we could. My father was really happy. He told me, 'Good job, Reneboy.'"

The pawnbroker gave Reneboy almost twenty dollars. The next day, the family gathered in front of the little hut built from four pieces of plywood in order to attend the momentous occasion of covering the façade with cement. When the work was finished, Edelberto said it looked like a real house, maybe not enough to revive a dream that had been dead and buried for a good while now, but enough to make him think that God hadn't forgotten about them. The next day, they went to the church to give thanks.

In the Philippines, there's a church and a fast food restaurant on every corner, the legacy of what Filipinos describe as three centuries in a convent and fifty years in Hollywood, in reference to the occupations by Spanish and American colonizers that have muddled their identity. Soon after arriving, the first inhabitants of the Promised Land had already established a church. Whenever they go, the Chales dress in their best clothing. Fe polishes the shoes they pulled from the landfill, mends her husband's jacket, and sprinkles the children with the last drops from a bottle of cologne discarded by some Manila madam. Only Fe, in her imagination, can detect the scent of basil on her children amid the stink of decay that permeates the Promised Land. Fe needs the church so she can endure her life in the landfill; she needs to hear the priest say that something better is on its way. She lives without really living, always afraid the children are going to get sick from breathing in the toxic gas that emanates from the mounds of trash and saturates everything.

"We have to get out of here," she tells Edelberto sometimes.

"Get out? Where to?" he asks. "We've got nothing. At least here we have a house and enough to eat."

"You've seen what happens to the other children. Some of them have even died, they've gotten so sick. Lots of them are born with problems. And now this disaster. Any day there could be another collapse and we could get buried here."

"Maybe next year we'll get a little money," says Edelberto, letting Fe live with the hope that she won't end her days in the Promised Land.

The first pictures of children scrabbling in the landfills of Manila swept around the world in the 1980s because of the striking contrast between those images and those of the opulent lives of the Marcoses, the most famous, extravagant, and corrupt matrimonial dictatorship of the era. Ferdinand Marcos had been the most promising officer in the Philippine armed forces; Imelda Romuáldez, the winner of a Miss Philippines pageant. They met, fell in love, and realized they had a lot in common: neither of the two was able to choose between money and power. They decided to steal both.

The general and the spoiled daughter of the Philippine elite followed the tradition carried on by so many other tin-pot dictators, who gave their regimes names that suggested the arrival of a new era, something better and unfamiliar. Mao had introduced the fanatical politics that would lead his people to starvation with his call to begin anew with a "clean sheet of paper." In Indonesia, Suharto had started his New Order by eliminating thousands of opponents in the anti-communist witch hunt of the 1960s, and in Cambodia Pol Pot had reset the calendar to Year Zero before launching his genocide. The Marcoses called their political offspring the New Society.

But there was nothing new in those dictatorships. Eliminating anyone who thinks differently, keeping the money the people have entrusted to you for building schools, destroying your own country with foolish, megalomaniacal ideas—all of these are time-honored ways of prostituting power. The Marcoses merely refined the government's "reverse Robin Hood" system, stealing everything they could from the poor in order to give it to the rich—and keeping the biggest piece of the pie for themselves. The country, which in the 1960s had become Asia's second most powerful economy after Japan, was plunged into a spiral of corruption and graft whose bill is still being paid by its people.

Imelda always struck me as the more interesting of the two. Years after she'd been ousted from power, she agreed to let me interview her in her apartment in Makati. She greeted me by saying, "Buenos días," using the Spanish that some of Manila's elite still speak in an effort to distinguish themselves from the masses, and then took my hand and led me toward one of the huge windows in her apartment.

"My dear," she said, gazing like a smitten adolescent at Ferdinand, who since his death had motionlessly presided over the living room in bust form, his World War II medals hanging around his neck. "Everything you see here, the two of us built together."

There I was being served tea by the woman who had once had the leaders of the world at her feet. Castro said she was the only lady in the world—apart from his mother—whom he had taken out for a drive through Havana. She danced with Ronald Reagan and sang for the leaders of the Soviet Union. She was the most attractive first lady of the twentieth century and the source of some of the most frivolous quotations in history ("If you know how much you've got, you probably haven't got much."). By now, though, she'd become a melancholy, bored grandmother. Together we watched videos of her official trips, dusted off photos of her engagement to Ferdinand, and reread old love letters. She noticed I couldn't help looking at her feet.

"My dear, I see you're staring at my shoes."

"It's inevitable, Madame."

"All right, I'll tell you about the shoes, if you're interested."

"Yes, of course I'm interested."

"Those savages who attacked our house [the presidential palace stormed by the demonstrators who brought down the Marcoses in 1986] were looking for skeletons in my closet, but they only found shoes, very pretty shoes. I was lucky in a way, don't you think?"

"Yes, but the people were starving and Madame had 1,220 pairs of expensive shoes in her closet. Wasn't that a bit much?"

"When I went to visit a king, I spent an hour getting dressed. When I was going to visit a slum, I'd spend two hours. I was like a movie star for the poor, and I gave them all my love. I was a mother to them. More tea?"

The Philippine elite, to which Imelda belongs, has always been a real cancer on the nation. Some of the richest families owe their position to their Spanish colonialist lineage, others to political power, and a very few to their effort and hard work. All of them maintain that position at the expense of the little people, opposing any reform that might give others a chance and controlling the levers of power to perpetuate what has become a monarchy in which money determines a person's position forever. The members of the Makati club see money as a divine right that should be passed down from generation to generation, one that belongs to them alone. In this exclusive club, the woman all get plastic surgery at the same clinic and the men all buy the same luxury cars; the children play in their own basketball league, and the young only marry members of other club families. The favored pastime is politics, and the club's members control the Senate and Parliament, many of the judgeships, and, except on those few occasions when an actor manages to sneak by them, the presidency too. The poor, they believe, are poor by divine will the same way the rich are rich, and it makes no sense to try to change something that's born in the blood. The poor are members of another dynasty, just a less fortunate one. The golden rule, which is rigidly obeyed and passed down through the generations: never feel guilty.

I was invited once to attend a dinner organized by Imelda Marcos's public relations arm in Manila's Shangri-La Hotel. A number of the most prominent members of the Makati monarchy were there. Seated at my table were a number of diamond-draped women and a few businessmen. Some asked about my work, and I decided to tell them the story of Dalmazio Zeta, a man I'd met in Tondo, one of Manila's most violent and impoverished neighborhoods. Dalmazio had an empty cookie box where he kept a list of the neighbors who were willing to sell a kidney for money. Every once in a while, the organ traffickers would show up, select one of the youngest on the list, and arrange the operation. The recipient, always a member of a wealthy Manila family, collected a new life from the most impoverished families and then headed back to his club; in exchange, the donor got enough to pay for a few creature comforts. I thought it a perfect example of the way the Philippine elite literally live off the poor. Some of my dinner mates did express real surprise that such a thing could be happening not far from where we were being served lobster and champagne, but finally one woman brought the conversation to a close in flawless Spanish:

"Isn't it amazing how generous people are? It just goes to show that Filipinos are not a resentful people."

It didn't take much effort to find more dignity in the Promised Land than at the dinner parties of the elite. The avalanche of garbage has been so devastating for the people of Payatas not just because of the loss of life and home, not even because it demonstrates just how abandoned they are, but because it came at a time when the residents were starting to believe that they had turned their leftover city into a place of which they could be proud.

Everything had started to change for the better in 1993, when the residents joined together to form the Payatas Scavenger Association in an attempt to fight for their rights. The local school was up and running at last. Even though weeks sometimes went by in which the teacher, driven off by the stench, failed to show up to work, the community was filled with satisfaction by the sight of the children walking to school dressed in their spotless uniforms, which had been conscientiously washed by their mothers the night before. Some of the shanties were improved and the roads, grown muddy during the monsoon, were paved. The streets between the mountains of garbage were cleaner than the avenues of Manila, and in the afternoon women could be seen sweeping outside, an image that might be startling in an endless sea of rubbish, but spoke to their desire to reclaim a little space from the filth.

Among the improvements carried out was a campaign to register its inhabitants with the government. It has always been important, in the sheet metal and cardboard slums, to have one's papers in order. Without them, the residents can't go to the hospital, file a lawsuit, enroll their children in public school, apply to most jobs, legally marry, inherit their parents' poverty, or vote. The police can do whatever they want to them, since on paper they don't exist. Now that they've been registered, the inhabitants of the Promised Land have overnight become a force to be reckoned with. Politicians have to hold their noses at election time and go to the landfill to ask for their votes. Shouldn't getting a whiff of poverty be among the required activities for any elected official?

Politicians have made a lot of promises in the Promised Land, but the residents only trust one of them: Joseph Estrada, the former actor and playboy who occupies the presidency. The poor see in their bacchanalian leader the character he played in the movies, always ready to defend the defenseless and confront the powerful in a country where such a thing could only take place in fiction. "This guy is different," they say. "He lived in a shanty, too," they recall, "and had to work hard before he made it big and escaped from poverty. He's a thief? Well, it's about time one of our people did some of the stealing." Estrada won the 1998 elections with the highest level of support ever seen in the country's democratic history, thanks in part to his humble origins.

When the great mountain tumbled down, the residents of Payatas hoped that the president would leap from the silver screen and come to their rescue. But the leader—their leader—has long since forgotten his origins. He spends much of his time trying to win over the people in the Makati monarchy, a group who have never accepted him and are just waiting for a chance to kick him out. Estrada is not one of them and never will be, no matter what he does. The president promised to compensate the victims of the disaster, get all of them back to work, and close the landfill, but in five months he has only managed to fulfill the last of his promises. For a time, the trucks no longer arrive in the Promised Land and the authorities search in vain for another place to dispose of Manila's scraps. The metropolis is turning into a landfill: the garbage accumulates in its streets and the mountains in Payatas begin to shrink. Is it possible that one day the inhabitants of the Promised Land will climb to the top of Mount Rubbish and see immense mountains of waste covering the city that never accepted them?

Some of the inhabitants of the Promised Land are offered construction jobs in the provinces, but people are afraid to leave and give up the only security they've attained in life. The dollar, the one dollar you have to earn even when everything falls apart around you, is harder to come by now. People start to despair. The scavengers association goes up in arms, they hold endless meetings that go past midnight. They debate what to do, how to make a living now, until one day, three months after the moratorium was declared, the majority votes to demand that the garbage return. They march to the offices of the city government with placards that say, "Who will feed our children? Save the poor. Bring the waste back." Government officials, who have taken a drubbing in the city's growing garbage crisis, stare at each other, astonished. They can't believe their luck. Are they really being asked to start drowning the people in garbage again? What is government for, if not to fulfill its citizens' wishes?

The day the trucks return, with the resolute pace of an invincible army, they are greeted by shouts of joy. Hundreds of residents are waiting, hooks and bags at the ready, and after the first truck dumps its contents, everyone rushes toward the waste as if, in a hallucination worthy of Don Quixote, it were a pool of clean, clear water. They see treasures where anybody else would see only garbage, food where there are only scraps, survival where there is only sickness. And everything goes back to the way it was. President Estrada goes to bed drunk at four in the morning, just as Reneboy is leaving the house to go earn a living.

"Did you fill your bag, Reneboy?"

But neither Reneboy nor the president is the same after Manila's "garbage war." The boy has lived without hope that the trucks might arrive. He's lived without diving into the mud of Mount Rubbish, and gone to school in the mornings and headed to bed as hungry as always, but cleaner than ever. In his free time, he and his friends have gone to Quezon City, not far from the Promised Land, and used the money they collected panhandling at intersections to treat themselves to soda and a little food. For the first time, he can imagine what life would be like far from here.

The president doesn't know it, but he has changed, as well. Joseph Estrada has had the chance to present himself as the defender of the poor. His failure to improve the lives of those who launched him into the presidency, to alter their fate in the least, has made him even more vulnerable in the eyes of the elite. And so, while the big city starts dumping whatever it doesn't need onto the people of the Promised Land, Manila also conspires to dump its president onto a political trash heap.

Fifteen years have passed since the ouster of the Marcoses, and Cardinal Sin, the man most responsible for the end of the dictatorship, has lost patience with the peccadilloes of the actor now dabbling in politics, with his dalliances and his cabinet meetings in which Johnnie Walker makes most of the decisions. Accusations of corruption pile up, and the institutional response falls short. The Church manages to bring together Manila's middle class; the business community, which sees a long-anticipated opportunity to kick the president out; the political opposition; and the military.

Watching the demonstrators march through the streets of Manila, it is clear to me that nobody in the Philippines has ever read a manual on how to start a revolution. There is no rage in their faces; it is quite possible that Filipinos take themselves less seriously than any other nation on earth. The demonstrators have decided to toss out their president by singing songs, wearing costumes, going out to eat on the sidewalks, and arranging protests through text messages, making this the first political unrest organized by cell phone. Cardinal Sin, the vice president and future leader Gloria Macapagal Arroyo, and General Reyes hold hands on EDSA, a symbol of the power of the people where the Marcos dictatorship was buried, and celebrate the downfall of the president of the poor. The John Wayne of Manila sobs like a little boy in his office, alone and clinging to a bottle of whisky. One of his aides enters the room and tells him it's time to leave the presidential palace.

"What did I ever do to the people?" Estrada blubbers, his head on his desk.

The elite is happy, having put one of its own in power once more: Arroyo, a princess of the Makati monarchy. The generals are satisfied, having demonstrated that they're still in charge. And the cardinal is delighted, too, as the Church has been shown to be above all good and evil in the Philippines.

Some people, though, are not content. The poor feel betrayed— one of their own won't be doing the stealing now—and even threaten to reinstall the ex-president in power. Some residents of the Promised Land get together and send a small troop of demonstrators to assist with the counterrevolution. They still love Estrada, despite his false promises. Seeing him brought low—a feeling they know all too well—they forgive him for not coming to their rescue when they needed him most. The police drive them back to their shacks with clubs and meet little resistance. Even the most illiterate peasant from the poorest country in the world knows it's unlikely that his future hangs on who holds the presidency.

As the protests fade, once again I leave the same old wounded Philippines. On the plane back to Hong Kong, I run into my friend Pekka Mykkanen, a correspondent from the Finnish paper *Helsingin Sanomat* with whom, months later, I will wander the streets of Islamabad looking for a place that serves vodka on the eve of the war in Afghanistan. Pekka sits down beside me, orders a drink from the flight attendant, and, leaning back in his chair, says, "Isn't this job incredible? We were just in a fucking revolution."

After a pause, he adds, "Everything changes to stay the same."

As the car heads into the streets of the Promised Land, the unmistakable smell of absurdity creeps in the same way it did the day I met Reneboy. I think back on the time that has passed. Five years is a long time anywhere, but in the Promised Land it's an eternity. I have the feeling that I've made this same journey before, just a few months ago, when I went to look for Vothy in the Russian hospital in Cambodia. Then, though, I was looking forward to finding the little girl in the pink dress to confirm she'd survived. Now I want just the opposite. Only if I don't find Reneboy here where I left him can I hope that his life has changed, that perhaps he's gone far away from this place to reverse the course of his life.

On the way to the landfill, I've been imagining different possibilities. I've settled on one in which I arrive at the Chale family's shanty and, when I ask about Reneboy, they tell me that he and the rest of his family left the Promised Land a long time ago. Edelberto found work in Mindanao and took everyone back to where he was born, intoxicated by the memory of the scent of coconut palms and salty ocean breezes where pirates still rule the waters, far from Manila, which had never even invited him in the door. "Fe, we're leaving," he would have told his wife. "I'd rather suffer the indignity of going home empty-handed than the humiliation of watching my children living off other people's scraps."

Mount Rubbish still rises just where I left it. At its base I run into a resident who's spent the past few years going from house to house to make a list of missing people in the garbage landslide. Are any of your children missing? Did you lose a spouse, a sibling, a cousin?

"There are at least a thousand," he tells me, rejecting the official figure of 219 dead. "They think we're too stupid to realize whether we've lost one of our children. They're still there, under the garbage."

The waste now arrives in more measured quantities so that the mountains don't get too high and collapse again in the monsoon rains. Some families, those that live closest to possible disaster, have been relocated to Montalban, a neighboring community. Mount Rubbish is still tall, but the monsoon has yet to arrive. From the top, it seems like time has stopped. In the distance, the city looks as close as ever—and just as far. Another planet. The trucks keep moving toward the Promised Land, where people are waiting for them. I look around me from on high and realize I could start over: I could choose one of the boys digging through the garbage and tell his story. He would get up at four in the morning, trying to fill his bag; he'd dream of driving one of those trucks and go to bed with an empty stomach. It's not poverty that makes some places especially unjust, but rather poverty's excruciating lethargy, its unshakeable calm, the assumption that nothing is going to change, the feeling that no matter how hard you swim, you'll always be adrift on a sea of infinite despair. It's not poverty, but poverty's quiet. Its motionlessness.

I can't pick out Reneboy from the boys around me. I try to remember the route he took when he guided me to his shack on the day we met. I make my way down the hill and at the foot of Mount Rubbish, dwarfed by the immensity of the mountain, I find the Chales' little hut, the one that, thanks to a gold necklace sold to a pawnbroker, has been faced with cement. There's no one inside. I ask the neighbors, and a woman tells me that the family has moved, though not as far as I'd imagined. She leads me down the main street, through the fish market and its flies, past the church and the cheerful political posters promising great changes. At the end of the street is an incline that leads to a plateau and, among the scrub, a shack.

"They live there," the woman says.

A little boy with brown skin and protruding ears opens the door. He stands silent a moment, then smiles and says, "The foreigner." Five years have passed, but Reneboy hasn't grown that much. His body is still that of a boy, now in the skin of a fifteen year old.

Fe is by the fire, boiling rice. The last few years since the tragedy have been difficult, Fe says, but Reneboy has worked hard. His little sister helps him and the older siblings are all married or have simply gotten as far away from this place as they can. They occasionally send an envelope with a little money, which has allowed the family to move into this new hut, which is a little farther away from the garbage and has a view of the great mountain. All the walls are cement and the roof is made of sheet metal. There are rats, but not as many. The Promised Land still lives up to its name . . . in the dark of night.

Reneboy tells me he no longer wants to drive a garbage truck and announce his arrival on the horn, bearing new treasures for everyone.

"When I turn sixteen, I'll join the army and leave here for good," he says, looking to Edelberto for approval.

Just as his father had in his youth, Reneboy now has a dream. It's decided: he'll leave this place, take the train, and get as far away as he can, in search of his own Promised Land.

Teddy

They've gathered around the corpse, but nobody knows what to do with it. Teddy Mardani, dead of a gunshot wound in the side, is the only proof that the soldiers have used real bullets against them. There in Jakarta's Atma Jaya University they carry Teddy to one of the classrooms and hastily set up a sort of morgue. A few students sing a patriotic hymn about fallen heroes while a girl with long black hair, tears in her eyes, writes on the blackboard the names of those who have died in the latest day of protests against the government. Sigit, Lukman, Muzamil, Noerma, Heru, Teddy Mardani . . .

There's a discussion about who should call Teddy's parents and what to tell them. Just a few hours ago, these students fearlessly faced down thousands of armed soldiers, but now, with that call looming, they pace nervously back and forth, arguing like children and making excuses to get out of the dreaded task.

"We have to tell them the truth," says one of them, raising his voice above his companions'.

"We should just tell them he is wounded," another responds.

"But he's dead, isn't he?" says a third.

"We'll say he died instantly."

Is it even possible to die instantly? Doesn't there have to be a fraction of a second, a tiny fragment of time between the moment we're struck by a bullet and the moment we fall to the ground, in which we know it's all over? Dying instantly. Is that really any better? Departing in total ignorance, without the chance to bid ourselves farewell or to give our executioner a last look that will haunt him as he stays among the living.

Only a few hours earlier, Teddy doesn't think dying is an option. Life hasn't yet shown him that bad things can happen to anyone; his ignorance keeps him from being afraid. A young student at Indonesia's Institute of Technology, he has joined together with his comrades from other universities to march on Parliament, demanding real democratic reforms and the removal of the military from politics. The police blockade the streets two kilometers away, at Semanggi Bridge in the city center. Security forces are arrayed like old-fashioned battle formations. On the front lines are riot police with tear gas, shields, and wooden clubs; behind them, police officers armed with automatic weapons; and behind them, soldiers from the Special Forces, with armored personnel carriers and assault rifles. The soldiers are the only ones who have permission to shoot if the front lines cannot hold. They've been granted impunity, and they're accustomed to taking advantage of it.

The students' formation is somewhat more chaotic. Everybody wants to be in front. They're also armed to the teeth—with flags, placards, and megaphones. When the two groups meet face to face, the students mock the soldiers and their weapons. One young man climbs on top of an old bus and shouts down at them. "Go home, don't obey anyone who tells you to fire on the people. Who do you think the people are? The politicians who spend their days warming the seats in Parliament with their farts, or us? Join us and fight!"

The hours pass, and students and soldiers continue to face off. The students want to get by, but the soldiers have orders to block their way. This lack of communication is striking, since the soldiers and students are the same age: some of them are just adolescents, seventeen or eighteen years old, and most are around twenty. The life of one of those soldiers wouldn't have had to change much at all for him to be standing beside the students now, and vice versa. If the parents of one of the soldiers had just been able to scrape together enough money to pay for university, he might not have had to look to the barracks for a way out.

When night comes, the soldiers are tired. The shields, armor, and weapons are heavy. The officers haven't eaten and their mood has soured over the course of the afternoon. An officer with a spotless uniform and medals on his chest picks up a megaphone and announces, "Anyone who isn't a member of the armed forces or the press corps must leave this place at once. I repeat, anyone who isn't a member . . ."

Another voice issues from among the group of students: "Maintain your positions."

A little while later, teargas starts billowing toward the students. The air of Jakarta suddenly tastes like pepper and garlic. I've tasted it before. At night, when I go back to the Le Meridien Hotel to write about the demonstrations, the gas creeps into my room through a drafty window while I watch police officers and university students chasing each other down Jenderal Sudirman Street. My eyes are tearing up, my computer screen is blurred, and I have to keep splashing my face with water.

The students have their own system for fending off the effects of the tear gas: they cover their mouths with their handkerchiefs and smear toothpaste around their eyes to soothe the stinging. They sing: *"Press on without tears / defending truth / Press on without fear / defending truth . . ."*

Trucks with high-pressure hoses arrive, and the water beats down on the students. They fall like dominoes but get up again and keep marching. They sing: *"We will press on together / we are devoted to you / our motherland."*

The police lines have broken; those of the students—if they were ever organized at all—are broken, as well. A few soldiers from the last line of defense, the only ones authorized to shoot to kill, take position in front, kneeling and taking aim at those enemies who might easily have been themselves. The soldiers have been told that they're something else entirely. In the barracks somewhere, they've cultivated the fantasy that dangerous enemies of the state are amassed where I see only unarmed youths. When they aim, they don't see people; they see the enemy.

A few shots ring out, and the crowd scatters in all directions. Some students fall to the pavement and lie there, still wearing their backpacks. The cry of *Reformasi* that has driven them throughout these long months of conflict now sounds timid and faltering amid the cries for help in the chaos. The last time they saw him, Teddy was running like the others, his back to the soldiers, leaping over burning tires and disappearing into the fog of tear gas, his face covered with the red-and-white Indonesian flag. When the night breeze clears the smoke, the students have lost their position and the soldiers are laughing and dancing in victory.

And Teddy? Has anybody seen Teddy Mardani?

They've gathered around the corpse, but nobody knows what to do with him. Ace and I arrived at Atma Jaya University unaware that we are the solution to the students' problem. Ace emigrated to Spain during the Franco dictatorship and spent a few years working in a Chinese restaurant on the Costa del Sol. When he returned to Indonesia, he found a job at the Spanish embassy in Jakarta. Together, on the back of his motor scooter, we've been to all the demonstrations, passing through military checkpoints with the help of my expired Spanish ID card as we follow the student protests around the capital city. Ace laughs when I tell him that if he were a little uglier and I a little prettier, we could pretend we were Guy Hamilton (Mel Gibson) and Billy Kwan (Linda Hunt) in *The Year of Living Dangerously*. We journalists love Peter Weir's film, which is based on the events that carried General Suharto to power. In it, the profession looks as adventurous and romantic as we all dreamed it would be in college, before realizing how different it can be in the real world. "You for the words, me for the pictures. I can be your eyes," Kwan tells Hamilton in the movie. Ace takes care of getting us through all the checkpoints, translating from Bahasa, and getting my photos developed. I take care of inviting him to dinner at the Lebanese restaurant at the Le Meridien, which reminds him of the Mediterranean.

The students greet us excitedly.

"*Wartawan, wartawan!*" they shout the word for journalist.

They take me to Teddy Mardani and remove the white sheet covering his corpse. They point to the bullet wound in his side and ask me to take a photo. I do, and they all sigh with relief, knowing that the evidence of the unevenness of their confrontation with Indonesian security forces has been recorded. The next day, the newspaper will publish the photograph with a caption that says the photo shows that the army "is using real bullets" against the unarmed students. Teddy has stood up for the cause to the end—and beyond. Now he can be laid to rest.

The friends of the dead student finally work up the nerve to call his parents, telling them their son has been shot by the army and died instantly. At the other end of the line, silence. When he comes to see his son's corpse, Mr. Samsudin doesn't make a fuss. He doesn't shed a single tear or ask whose fault it is. Nor does he swear revenge. He stands quietly beside the body, closes his eyes a few seconds, and says, "God must have wanted it this way."

Teddy Mardani's funeral takes place in Jakarta's Karet Cemetery on November 15, 1998, two days after his death. It is attended by his parents, Edi and Maria Samsudin; his three sisters, Rifa, Lin, and Yuli; the director and professors from his college; and nearly three thousand students wearing the colors of the different Indonesian universities. Teddy's best friends toss flower petals on his grave. When the gravediggers move in to finish their work, Maria Samsudin shatters the silence of the cemetery with her sobbing, and her daughters have to restrain her so she doesn't throw herself into the grave with her son. The students wait motionless for the Samsudin family to depart so they can bid their comrade farewell in their own way. They haven't just come to say goodbye to Teddy: they're here to show that their cause lives on without him, that no matter how many funerals they attend, no matter how many of their schoolmates they say goodbye to, nobody can bury their cause. His voice trembling at seeing a mother in pain, a mother who might have been his own, one student cries out for the succor that some of them feel is lacking.

He shouts that God is great: *"Allahu Akbar."*

"Allahu Akbar," they all repeat.

Only a few months before, Jakarta's university students achieved something unimaginable. After weeks of protests, in a revolt organized in the classrooms, they occupied the parliament building in May 1988 and forced General Suharto to step down. The dictator who had ruled over the Indonesian people for three decades, commander of the largest army in Southeast Asia, was shown up by a bunch of kids with tousled hair and big ideals. The students had been born under his dictatorship, they'd never known anything else, and they certainly hadn't suffered it the way their parents had. It is surprising, then, how naturally they have accepted the possibility that they might die for democracy, even though they've never experienced the concept firsthand and would be hard-pressed to miss it. That's the way it always goes: young students, free of their elders' apprehensions, try to bring change to tyrannized countries, risking not only the lives they're living now but the many years that lie ahead of them. Sometimes, as when the dictators in Beijing directed tanks to Tiananmen Square, or when Burmese generals crushed the democratic protests in Rangoon in August 1988 and September 2007, the sacrifice is especially painful. The brave effort, the loss of life—they do nothing to bring about change, and the dictators remain in power. Generations must pass until, once the memory of the brutal past has faded and fear has diminished, other students head out into the streets again.

The Indonesian university students are worried that theirs has been yet another revolution that couldn't. Suharto has fallen, yes, but his regime is still standing. The new president charged with carrying out the transition to democracy is Suharto's right-hand man, Habibie. The head of the armed forces responsible for the students' deaths, General Wiranto, still has his job. The economic elite that has sacked the country retains its privileges, and Suharto has simply retired to his Jakarta mansion. He has received the kind of cushy retirement that dictators who once served at the pleasure of the West are so often granted. Veteran human-rights activist Reed Brody once described this situation with a simple mathematical equation: "If you kill one person, you go to jail; if you kill twenty, you go to an institution for the insane; if you kill twenty thousand, you get political asylum." If, furthermore—as in the case of Indonesia's "smiling general"—you mismanage billions of dollars, divvy up the nation's wealth among your children, and invade and destroy a country such as East Timor, then, with all those achievements to your name, you will be allowed to retire and enjoy your fortune in peace. Nobody will bother you.

Teddy Mardani and his comrades feel that they've been deceived and decide to continue their demonstrations. They set up what they call the "central command" in an old science classroom in Atma Jaya University. They have a computer, a radio, a telephone, supplies, and maps to coordinate the protests. The People's Consultative Assembly, a legislative body composed of soldiers and members of the old regime, plans to meet to trace out the path to democracy after the fall of the general. Among other things, however, the body is expected to allow generals to retain their permanent seats in the assembly, which means the military will retain its grip on national politics. The students paint new placards, take up collections to rent buses, and decide to head for Parliament to demand the dismantling of the old regime that has so far refused to die, the expulsion of the army from politics, and a trial for General Suharto. But the street has been blocked at Semanggi Bridge, and at dusk the air fills with the taste of pepper and garlic.

And Teddy? Has anybody seen Teddy Mardani?

Perhaps it is possible to fall in love with a country the way you might with a person, to see in it things that, for whatever reason, you don't find in any other; to have a special connection with it, to be drawn to its character, to live it with an extraordinary intensity. These countries take advantage of your smitten state, so that you fail to notice their defects and constantly encounter their virtues. You dream of returning to them before you've even left. Indonesia, for me, is that country. When I arrive in Indonesia, I know I couldn't possibly be anywhere else: they could blindfold me, and no sooner had I set foot in one of its airports than I would recognize where I was just from the spicy-sweet scent of clove cigarettes and frangipani perfume. Indonesia has a hidden side that makes its people unpredictable, a side I find unsettling and fascinating at once. The best and worst of the human condition are often crudely apparent here, where in other places our virtues and faults, while just as present, have been masked by time and polished by convention. In Indonesia, I have witnessed the most savage violence—the decapitations of the Madurese in Borneo, the final spasms of a man beaten to death by a mob in the streets of Jakarta—and I've seen places innocent of politics and cynicism, such as the dominion of the Badui in the Kendeng Mountains of Java, where the descendants of the princess Pajajaran cling to a life without government, television, or materialism. Not even the General dared to interfere there, wary of the superstition that says that terrible illnesses will befall anyone who disrupts Badui territory. Suharto, who invaded and conquered, pilfered and destroyed so many places, never dared set foot in their forest, though it lay only a hundred kilometers from his Jakarta palace.

Indonesia's singularity must have something to do with the violent origins of this land, which is split into thousands of islands that emerged thousands of years ago from an explosion in the bowels of the Earth. It must have been a difficult birth, and it produced so many islands that the rulers of the largest archipelago in the world have long wondered how many pieces of land they had under their domain. Dutch colonizers made the first count, totting islands up by hand from the decks of their ships; it's no surprise that their figure was off by thousands. Later, cartographers were sent up in little planes to mark down the islands they saw from the air, which seemed to total some thirteen thousand. As aircraft and cartography methods advanced and the latest satellite photography systems came into use, modern cartographers concluded that Indonesia has exactly—at least until the next inventory—17,508 islands inhabited by about 300 ethnic groups speaking 583 different languages and dialects.

General Suharto has always thought of all this diversity as a marvelous puzzle that can entertain him during those times when he isn't otherwise occupied with stealing from his citizens or eliminating his political enemies. Influenced by the migration policies established by the Dutch colonizers and by Sukarno, the founder of the nation, Suharto came up with the most remarkable and destructive of all his ideas: why not relocate millions of inhabitants from Java, Indonesia's largest island and the center of power, to the remotest reaches of the nation? The tribes in Sulawesi, Sumatra, and Borneo would become civilized, the country would be united under Javanese influence, and the population and resources would be more evenly distributed.

In Madura, a poor, arid island off the east coast of Java, it was not hard to find volunteers ready to begin a new life in distant Borneo. Madurese immigrants started arriving in Borneo through a program that promised them a job, free schooling for their children, a piece of land, and the administration's favor. Given these government advantages, the new arrivals quickly established profitable businesses and became the dominant class. Javanese also arrived from other parts, creating Madurese businesses and felling the forests, which the Dayaks, the principal native tribe, consider sacred. The indigenous population watched powerless as its ancestors' jungles were destroyed and highways were hacked through them. New factories went up outside the villages, and the neon lights of the karaoke clubs illuminated the nights where before only the glow of bonfires could be seen.

At the beginning of the '90s, the Dayaks began to rebel against the changes around them, massacring Madurese immigrants every three or four years. Tensions between natives and immigrants rose, and finally the Dayaks decided that the time for the final solution had come. All the men claimed to have received instructions from their imaginary commander-in-chief, the hornbill with feathers in the impossible hues of the rainbow that had summoned their parents and their parents' parents to war. If any of them doubted that the chief was real—and something that wasn't real would be hard pressed to order a genocide—they didn't speak up. That night the Dayaks sharpened their knives, tied machetes to bamboo poles, daubed their arrows with poison, drank themselves into a stupor, and promised their supreme chief, the protector spirit of the Borneo jungle, that they would carry out its orders. The others had to die. The women and children of the others had to die, their properties had to burn, and any who managed to escape had to have no reason to return, since they would dwell in nothingness from now on.

And everything would go back to the way it was before they arrived.

The others realized it was time to flee when they spotted the first decapitated heads floating by their villages, pulled along on the current of the Sampit River. Some ran for the jungle, but nobody knows the jungle better than a Dayak. They were hunted down like animals. Some packed up their possessions and tried to escape by road to the coast, thinking that perhaps the Dayaks wouldn't have had time to block the way. They were dragged from their vehicles and massacred by the side of the road. The government sent in soldiers and police reinforcements, who promptly fled to save their own skins. There was no authority that could defend the Madurese, no witness ready to tell their story, no international television channels willing to describe their woes, and so they were systematically eliminated. This was Indonesia at its most primitive and savage. It was the early days of 2001, the beginning of the new century. How was it possible?

When I arrive in Palangkaraya, the capital of Central Kalimantan, one of the four provinces of Indonesian Borneo, the indigenous tribes have piled up dozens of skulls in the basement of what used to be the Rama Hotel. Lying on the roadway at one entrance to the city are the bodies of two little girls, five and six years old, their heads separated from their trunks like broken dolls, a childish expression still on their faces, their hair disheveled and their eyes wide, as if only at the last moment had they understood that none of it was a game.

The Dayaks decapitate their victims, drink their blood, and eat their hearts, believing that at every feast they increase their powers and honor their invisible commander. A dozen warriors, armed with poison darts, spears, and machetes, greet me. The eyes of Acuk, their leader, are bloodshot with rage. When he sees me, his expression changes and he smiles. It's hard to understand how men who yesterday were carpenters, mechanics, taxi drivers, and fathers can today be counting the number of neighbors they've killed and arguing among themselves about who's eaten more hearts and should therefore lead the next attack. I ask Acuk whether he feels regret when he surveys all that death and desolation.

"The others must die," he replies.

Later, after telling me in detail how he's been eating only his victims' flesh for days, Acuk leans on my shoulder and asks me if I'd like to stay to dinner. It's clear that he understands that my menu should consist of "normal food," maybe a bit of fried rice with chicken, but I can't bear the thought of it.

"I'm sorry, I'm not hungry," I say, trying not to be sick.

"Tomorrow, then?" he asks.

"Maybe some other time . . . "

If the anthropologists who have studied the Dayaks agree on anything, it's that, their cannibal past now behind them, they are one of the friendliest, most welcoming communities on earth. Why, then, has the dark side of the legendary headhunters of Borneo returned, nearly two centuries after they greeted the first Western diplomatic delegation by decapitating Dutch officer George Muller on the banks of the Kapuas River? Has nothing changed in all this time, even though parabolic antennas perch atop the natives' huts and the Christian missionaries have managed to get them to attend mass on Sundays?

Or maybe that's the problem: everything has changed.

Ensconced in his Jakarta mansion and enjoying the sort of retirement reserved for those who have slaughtered enough people to avoid jail or the insane asylum, Suharto watches his Indonesian puzzle break into pieces. Ever since his deposal, different ethnic groups have been slitting each other's throats in the jungle, Muslims and Christians have been massacring each other in the Moluccas, separatists in Aceh and West Papua have been in revolt again, and Islamist terrorists have been blowing Bali nightclubs to smithereens. For decades the dictator was able to keep this pressure cooker of a country under control, but it is exploding now that he's fallen from power. Suharto is probably enjoying it all: he's one of those tyrants who invert good and evil in their minds until they become linked—as if by umbilical cords—to their own personal interests. He surely thinks that if the country falls apart, the people will long for the old days when he held it together and will cry out for him to restore the New Order. But the students with their endless demonstrations, which surround his mansion one day and the next take over the streets of Jakarta, are not about to allow anything of the sort.

There is one piece of the puzzle whose loss pains the general. The eastern half of the island of Timor was a colony of Portugal up until 1974, when the last Portuguese ships finally left. Suharto, armed with the blessing—and weapons—of the United States, decided to invade it shortly thereafter, and over the next quarter of a century his troops trampled the population while the rest of the world remained largely indifferent.

With Suharto out of power, the newly installed President Habibie is under pressure from the international community to demonstrate his commitment to human rights. In the summer of 1999, the Indonesian government decided to put the question to the Timorese themselves in a popular referendum: did they want to be part of Indonesia or become independent? For many locals, this was like asking whether they would extend a dinner invitation to the man who killed their father, raped their sister, and humiliated their family. I was unable to cover the day of the vote because it also happened to be the day of my wedding. So while I was saying "yes" to my fiancée, Carmen, in Madrid, East Timor was saying "no" to Indonesia. Both undertakings—my marriage and their divorce—would get off to a rough start.

The Indonesian army decided that if East Timor wasn't going to be theirs, it wasn't going to be anybody's. The destruction of the territory began while I was on the island of Lombok, sunbathing on Senggigi Beach and chugging down cocktails with names like Sex on the Beach and Tequila Sunrise. One afternoon I turned on the hotel television to watch the news, and there it was, the country that nobody had noticed for a quarter of a century, the top story on the networks. Leaders from all over the world were acting like they'd only found out yesterday that the Timorese were under assault. Pro-Indonesian militias and the army were destroying the country village by village, house by house. The United Nations, which had been on the island organizing the voting, did what it usually does in such situations: when things got ugly, it started evacuating its personnel and abandoned the Timorese to their fate.

The newspaper had been trying to track me down for days, knowing only that I was honeymooning on "an Indonesian island" near Timor. I felt like a firefighter who's still lounging by the pool while the house next door is in flames. Journalism has never been one of those professions where you can take off your uniform when you get home and put it back on when you're ready to punch in at the office the next morning. You're a journalist from the moment you get up to the time you go to bed at night. You can't simply opt for the privileges afforded by one of the best jobs in the world and reject its inconveniences. Still, couldn't it have all waited until my honeymoon was over?

There were still two days left of our trip, and Carmen had noticed my growing fretfulness.

"If you think you should go, go," she says.

"But it's our honeymoon," I answer, my mouth tight, "and we still have a couple of days left."

"If you stay, you're not going to enjoy it. Go on, just come back in one piece and we'll go again when you get back."

The next day we fly to Bali, where I hope to catch a flight to Kupang, the western capital of the island of Timor. All the seats on the day's only flight are full, and Carmen sighs, but then we learn that one of the passengers has overslept. There's one empty seat, and I hurry off to take it, promising as I leave to make it up to Carmen and then some. Little do I know that two days later I will be further than ever from being able to fulfill my promise. I will also have discovered that I'm not at all the hero I always envisioned in my fantasies of being a war reporter.

When you arrive at a story late, you've got to make up for lost time, but you don't know enough about the situation on the ground. Almost all the journalists who were covering the voting in Dili have now fled to Bali. I, on the other hand, find myself making the journey in the opposite direction. I arrive in Kupang and immediately cross the western side of the island to reach Atambua, a border town between the two Timors, and find a room in a tiny hotel on the main street. The pro-Indonesia militias have also chosen Atambua as their destination as they pull out of East Timor because of the imminent arrival of Australian troops. I request a room, and the hotel owner looks at me as if I'm speaking in Martian.

"You're the only Westerner here," he says. "Are you sure you want to stay?"

The only place in the whole town for making international calls is a single tiny call center—and it's not working. I have no cell phone coverage, and I can't get in touch with the newspaper. A few minutes after my arrival, the hotel is surrounded by militia members. As they've retreated, they've left hundreds of corpses in the streets of East Timor. One of the fighters is wearing a T-shirt from the Barcelona Football Club, and I decide that might be my chance to communicate. I go outside and show him my passport, which notes that I was born in Barcelona.

"Australian?" he asks.

"No, Spanish, from Barcelona."

"Australian," he repeats. "Death to Australians!"

"No, no, Spanish, from Barcelona," I try to explain. "In Spain, south of France, next to Portugal. In Europe . . ."

"Australian!" he declares.

I'm afraid that soon I won't be Spanish or Australian, but just a corpse. The hotel owner tells me to hide in my room, under the bed.

"They're coming for you," he says.

I peek out the window, and there they are, growing progressively more agitated. They're calling for death to the Australian: my supposed compatriots have become their favorite prey because they are preparing a military operation to end the violence. The militia arrives in stolen UN all-terrain vehicles, which are painted with slogans like "It's ours now" and "Come and get it!" Their weapons give the scene an unreal quality, as if they're from another era: they carry machetes, spears, even bows and arrows. For a moment, I imagine I'm in one of those Western movies I loved so much as a child, looking out the window at what could well be your typical Wild West saloon and watching those shirtless men surge around the hotel, shouting and cheering. John Wayne, in this situation, would have smoked a cigarette, checked to see how many bullets he had left in the chamber, and had a drink as he waited for the outlaws. I try to follow my host's advice and hide under the bed, but the space isn't big enough.

I am afraid.

It's an unfamiliar fear, one I've never felt since, even when covering other conflicts. Now, years later, I know too well that it's the fear you feel when you're certain your journey's come to an end. My legs are shaking, I aimlessly pace the room, and my thoughts clang around in my head. I think about all that I've always wanted to do and now never will. I think about Carmen and my family. I think about what the end will be like. Will it be quick? Or will they amuse themselves for a while before playing soccer with my Australian-from-Barcelona head?

Someone hammers on my door, and my heart seems to stop. They're here and now there's nothing I can do.

"Open up, we're here to save you."

Save me? I open the door and find a group of armed men standing outside it. They carry me off down the hall on their shoulders, protecting me with automatic rifles, and toss me in the back of a vehicle. We peel away, honking. I can still see the disappointed faces of the mob. The party is off; their prey has vanished. The owner of the hotel, whom I've never seen again and whose name I never had the chance to ask, saved my life with a last-minute call to a friend of his at the police station. Or maybe he was afraid they'd burn down his hotel with me in it, and he was saving his business, not me. I'll have to return to Atambua one of these days to ask him and give him my thanks.

Days later, I enter East Timor with the first Australian soldiers and a group of fellow journalists. I won't see such destruction again until the great Asian tsunami of December 2004 ravages the coasts along the Indian Ocean in one of the largest natural disasters of our times. All public buildings and houses without an Indonesian flag have been burned or lie in ruins. Later, when the damage is assessed, estimates suggest that eighty percent of the houses in the country have been destroyed. Thousands of people who have spent the last few days in hiding begin to emerge out of nowhere like ghosts and, after their initial shyness, cheer us on from the side of the road as we enter Dili. The country is in tatters, and the last Indonesian soldiers are waiting humiliated in the port to board their ships and leave this puzzle piece that's never really fit. Was Indonesia doomed to fall apart entirely? Was it another failed nation, born from the unnatural maps of colonial powers and megalomaniacal dictators? Could my beloved Indonesia be just another made-up country?

The days of revolution continued for a time. The students protested everything from the abuses in East Timor to corruption to the slow pace of democratic reforms, which, notwithstanding the students' impatience, were taking shape little by little. In those days, it seemed anything was possible, and on the monsoon afternoons it was as if opium was raining down on Jakarta. The city was temperamental, swinging from violence to jubilation in a matter of hours. For the university students, there were no limits: they felt powerful, able to bring to their knees the politicians who had oppressed the Indonesian people for so long. Forcing presidents to resign became their favorite extracurricular activity. The ouster of Suharto was followed by those of Habibie and, later, Abdurrahman Wahid, the country's first democratically elected president. The leaders of the first uprisings moved on, and the new students coming up in the ranks of the *Reformasi* movement joined not because of their hunger for freedom from the past but in order to make their mark in an era that was getting away from them. In truth, it was already over. Indonesian democracy, after a shaky start and a few moments of crisis, was moving forward. The country was holding the first democratic elections in its history, and for once I was visiting it without having to go to morgues or flee from tear gas. Teddy Mardani's comrades could look back and tell themselves it had all been worth it.

Over the years, Indonesia has continued to be the same special place to me it's always been, but our relationship has matured. Now it's more like a marriage that, though it's lost the spark of novelty, remains loving. I don't look wistfully back at the days gone by: even if they were full of adventure and excitement, they were difficult times for people I care about. Nothing is ever routine about my trips back to Indonesia. The only constant is the way the memories of Teddy Mardani and the students who risked all for democracy hit me every time I land in Jakarta.

The same could not be said of the Indonesian people. When I return to the country, I am struck by how many seem to have forgotten those who made a new dawn possible. The students who protested in 1998 have taken different paths. Some of them have joined the unemployment rolls, others have gotten married and started a family, and a few have taken the next step into politics, even joining Golkar, Suharto's old party, in exchange for a salaried job.

Yet what hurts the most isn't that the living have been forgotten but that the dead have, too.

The Mothers of Semanggi, a group established by the families who lost their children the night Teddy Mardani was killed, have tried to keep the memory alive. For years they've sought justice, trying in vain to have those responsible stand trial or to prosecute General Wiranto, who was head of the armed forces when the students were gunned down in the streets of Jakarta. The witness testimony, the ammunition used, the bodies' locations—it all points to the soldiers. The autopsy performed by one of Teddy's own sisters leaves no room for doubt: the bullet that killed him entered through his side and kept going through his body, piercing one of his lungs and perforating his bowels. They found it in his mouth. It was the same kind as those used by the Indonesian Special Forces.

The Mothers of Semanggi hold meetings, collect all the evidence, analyze documents, discuss what else they can do. Above all, they cry together, because they alone know how much the loss of a child hurts and how hard it is to keep going when those to blame for that child's death have not been held responsible. Their lives are on hold, and, though their children lie in the ground, they haven't been able to bury them.

Teddy Mardani's mother goes to the meetings in secret. Her husband doesn't know, and she doesn't say where she's been when she comes home. The family has been under strain after the death of their son. Everything the dead student's parents believed in has been upended by losing him. They are divided: Maria is convinced that the family cannot keep going without knowing the truth about what happened and seeing those responsible behind bars, while Edi wants to let things be. When I finally meet them, seven years after photographing their son's corpse, the wound is still fresh. It is as if time had stopped on that November day in 1998.

Mr. Samsudin greets me in pajamas, his mood somber and his face sad. The far wall of the living room is lined with photos of their dead son and, beside them, one of Captain Edi Samsudin in military dress, in better times.

"You were in the army?" I ask, surprised.

"Yes, for forty years," he answers. "I'm retired now."

It all makes sense; all my questions are answered. All these years, the captain has been trapped between his unshakeable loyalties: between the need to know who shot his son and his love for the army he served all his life, between the urge to seek the truth and his fear of finding it, between his memories of the son in whom he'd placed all his hopes and his feeling that somehow he'd been betrayed by him. His coldness at the sight of Teddy's corpse when he came to the university, the fact that he attributed his son's death to God, his refusal to investigate—it was all there in that image of the captain in uniform. Hadn't the army supported his family and given him an opportunity? Hadn't Suharto been a strong leader who'd made the world respect Indonesia? "These young people aren't satisfied with anything," he must have thought as he watched the demonstrations on television, not knowing his own son was among them.

After Teddy's death, while Maria sobbed and cursed the soldiers who'd shot at unarmed students in cold blood, Edi rejected all the evidence and forbade anyone in his home to accuse his comrades in arms again. Sitting in his living room, with the defeated look of someone who's lost interest in life, the captain tells me the arguments he's been constructing in his head to make his existence more bearable.

"Soldiers aren't the only ones who have guns," he says vehemently, mustering energy from somewhere in his frail body. "They say the army killed my son, but it could have been another demonstrator. Why should I believe what a bunch of delinquents say? My son never should have been there. They tricked him. Young people believe anything you tell them."

"The evidence seems to indicate that it was the soldiers."

"You know," the captain answers, his voice soft again, "I've served the army faithfully for many years, and there are people who try to convince me that my commanding officers were the ones who gave the order to fire at my son. I'm only going to say this once: it's not true. My son died because it was God's will, and we'll never know who shot him."

More than any of his comrades, Teddy Mardani might have been on the soldiers' side that day of the demonstration at Semanggi Bridge. The youngest of four siblings, the only son in a middle-class Jakarta family, he'd been living and breathing the military since he was a boy, attending parades and admiring his father's uniform. The captain spent most of his career in desk jobs, loyal to General Suharto to the end and always ready to be called to sacrifice for his country. He didn't consider it a stain on his honor that his presence had never been required on the battlefield, because, as he said, "It's in the rearguard that battles are won." Of course he wouldn't have minded if his son had come home from school one day and announced that he wanted to follow in his father's footsteps and join the army. The armed forces had made a man out of him when, still just a lad, he'd shown up at the barracks in Jakarta with the big dreams of someone who thinks he's found his place in the world. But Teddy told him he had other ideas, that he was going to build bridges and highways and help make Indonesia a modern, powerful country. The boy expressed enough patriotic enthusiasm to stave off any objections from his father; he was going to be a civil engineer.

Teddy had been outgoing and decisive ever since he was a child, offering to lead school groups in secondary school, and becoming vice president of the student council at his college. When the deaths of four students gunned down by security forces at Trisakti University sparked massive protests against Suharto, he decided to join the fight. He knew that it was a historic moment and believed that things might change. Every afternoon, he and other students met at the university and organized the protests with detailed maps of streets, bridges, and infrastructure that he had borrowed from the engineering school. He called other universities to coordinate the marches and collected funds for the placards and bus rentals.

When he arrived home and his parents asked him how his day had gone, he talked about studying, exams, and friends. He stayed quiet while his father complained about university students who are never satisfied. Teddy decided to spare him the unpleasant truth. His friends knew, which is why none of them had wanted to call their fallen comrade's house. How could they explain to the captain that his son had been at the confrontation at Semanggi?

Maria, on the other hand, had never cared that her son was participating in the demonstrations. She thought it was the decision of an idealistic, somewhat impetuous young man, a rash adventure that she attributed to his age. As she saw it, only the people who had pulled the trigger—and especially the one who'd given the order to fire—were to blame.

Every once in a while, in a fit of courage, she'd show her husband the latest findings gathered in the Mothers of Semanggi's investigations, but lately she'd stopped, since it only seemed to widen the chasm that had opened between them and to exacerbate the contradictions that tormented the captain. After all, it was the loyalty of soldiers like Mr. Samsudin that had allowed Suharto to remain in power for three decades. Asking him to change his mind now would be like asking him to renounce everything he'd been in life.

While the captain and I talk about his son, Maria appears in the living room every few minutes, leaving again when she catches her husband's disapproving glances. I've spoken to her by phone a few hours earlier, and she's happy that a journalist is still interested in what happened. She's told me that she will not give up until the guilty parties are brought to trial. Every time she comes to serve us more tea, she speaks to me with her eyes.

"Don't believe what you're hearing," they tell me. "It's not true. Edi isn't a bad man, just a tortured one. He knows who really killed our son."

Mr. Samsudin shows me the family photo album. He flips through the pages of the Samsudins' wedding day, the birth of their children, Teddy's high school graduation, and stops at a photo that takes up a whole page. It's General Wiranto saluting the captain in a photograph from happier times. The image occupies a place of honor among the family photos, presiding over the old soldier's memories.

I've been planning to tell Mr. Samsudin that I saw his son's body at the university, the first time I'd seen a person who'd been shot to death, and that I saw the other students honor him as a hero. I've been planning to tell him that the soldiers knelt at the front lines and fired on unarmed students, and that their comrades in arms cheered on every burst of gunfire, that they laughed and leaped, delighted to have brought those students down. And that it is the soldiers, and nobody else, who should feel shame over Teddy's death. And that Teddy's sacrifice was not in vain and Indonesia today is a stronger, more just country because of it. And that he can be proud of his son.

I hold back.

I look at the lost expression of a broken man as he clutches the album with a photo of him receiving a salute from the officer who gave the order to fire on his son, and I take my words with me, aware that on my next visit to Indonesia I'll still be haunted by the memory of Teddy and of that young woman with long black hair who wept as she wrote his name on a chalkboard at Jakarta's Atma Jaya University.

Mariam

Remembering the fear that had gripped me in that grimy hotel in Timor, wiping away all the courage I'd thought I had, and the way the Timorese had stoically endured it day after day over a quarter-century of Indonesian occupation, I began to think the world was divided by fears.

In a Western city, fear might be a dark, empty street we have to cross at night, one we'd like to illuminate by flipping a switch as if we were seated comfortably in our living rooms. Or it might be the possibility of a stock market crash, a lost job, or a girlfriend who doesn't love us back. These are fleeting fears, rarely threatening or dangerous. In truth, daily life doesn't offer us enough fear, which is why we occasionally go to the cinema hoping a good horror movie will make us feel it a little more.

In the countries that don't matter, fear doesn't come and go: it lives inside people from the time they get up to when they go to bed at night. It sticks to their skin from cradle to grave. In the Promised Land in the Philippines, fear is rats getting to the baby as it sleeps, so one of a family's most valuable possessions is a wicker basket to hang from the roof so the child can dream in suspended peace. In the villages of Cambodia, fear is stepping on one of the mines that litter the Kampuchea rice paddies, mementos of a time when brothers fought against brothers. In Afghanistan, fear is the simple noise of an airplane overhead. The same sound that we identify with vacations or visits from far-flung relatives reminds Afghan children of bombs, another attack—quick, get to safety! Mohamed Ayan, the old bellhop of the Intercontinental Hotel in Kabul, explained it to me once, stroking his long, thick beard, which has turned white as he's waited for the war to end: "In Afghanistan it rains more bombs than water."

The Hazara, one of Afghanistan's ethnic minorities, have gotten used to scanning the sky hoping for rain, only to find once more that the Sky God is dropping bombs again. Theirs is a land rarely graced by nature's virtues but frequently punished by the worst flaws of the human condition. The hot winds of the Indian monsoon are blocked by high peaks before they reach the Bamiyan Valley, in the heart of Afghanistan, and dampen only the eastern reaches of the country, leaving the villages of the central regions without enough water to feed their animals or water their fields. Because of the constant droughts, people have to walk several kilometers to find wells of potable water. They drink a small amount on their way back to the village and then offer the rest to the animals they depend on for survival. The whole valley has just one aging weather station; it has recorded an annual average of twenty days of rain over the last few decades. In a bad season, when months go by without a single drop of water falling, Mohamed Ayan's axiom literally becomes reality. More bombs rain than water.

The Hazaras have never understood why from the beginning of history they have had to not only contend with the harsh climate that already makes life so difficult, but to fend off others' efforts to complete the task that nature pursues with such determination. Their Mongoloid features, a souvenir of what some historians believe was the passage through their lands of Genghis Khan and his hordes; their round, ruddy cheeks and flat noses; their Shiite faith in a country that is predominantly Sunni—all of it makes the Hazaras easy to identify, separate, and eliminate. Every invader who's swept through the Bamiyan Valley has tried it, and some have nearly succeeded.

The Taliban are the latest to attempt to eradicate the Hazaras. They controlled Afghanistan from their rise to power in 1996 until their ouster in 2001. The Muslim fundamentalists find Hazara noses particularly significant because, they claim, they are suspiciously similar to those of the giant Buddha statues sculpted 1,500 years ago in the mountains of Bamiyan. According to the Taliban, their noses prove that the Hazaras' ninth-century conversion from Buddhism to Islam was a sham. They are still infidels.

Mariam has large, wide eyes, round cheeks, ruddy skin, and a nose . . . well, I couldn't say whether her nose resembles those of the giant Buddhas. Is it flat enough that she deserves to die? Prominent enough that she doesn't? The little Hazara girl was five years old when the Commander of the Faithful, Mullah Omar, occupied Kabul and made Afghanistan the worst place on earth to be a girl. Dolls and any other representation of the human form were prohibited, along with kite flying, television, painting, music, and smiling, an act considered too flirtatious for little girls. Mariam and other girls her age have learned not to smile. They hide their emotions, and it's hard to tell whether they're happy or sad, whether inside they're laughing or crying.

The Taliban also decided to close the schools. All girls were ordered to stay at home with the women. Once a week, Mariam covers her face and her uncle accompanies her to a secret school set up in the private kitchen of one of the women who lives in the town of Nayak, in the district of Yakawlang. The kitchen wasn't chosen as the improvised classroom by chance: if the agents of the Department for the Promotion of Virtue and Prevention of Vice show up at the house, the pencils and notebooks can swiftly be swapped out for aprons and saucepans. The women can say they're cooking, the only activity permitted them besides housekeeping and childrearing. Mariam goes back home when classes end at noon, and her mother asks her what she's learned at school.

"Nothing," she says. "It's hard to think because we're afraid they're going to catch us and punish us."

Mariam worries in the present, but she fears the future even more. Her future is clearly traced out in her mother, in the way she is beaten in the middle of the street when she goes out to do the shopping unaccompanied by a male family member, in the humiliations of a social structure that values animals over women, because women are, in the eyes of the Taliban, the crooked lines of humanity, an evil that corrupts men and makes them weak. The guardians of virtue have been trained in Koranic schools that have restricted their contact with women, including their mothers and sisters. Their repression of women is rooted in part in an unsettling fear of the unknown. The Taliban are also obsessed with little girls, since one day those girls will become women. The abolition of the condition of womanhood should begin in childhood, before the threat becomes a reality.

The children of Bamiyan might be able to distract fear for a while, but soon enough the noise of the mortars announcing a new assault—by rebels who claim to protect them from the Taliban? or by Taliban soldiers who claim to be protecting them from the rebels?—breaks up the scattered moments of normalcy. If the Taliban are in control, Mariam spends her days shut up at home, helping her mother in the kitchen and only going out when necessary. She is again confined to the house when the rebels retake the valley, because everybody knows that the government will launch a counterassault soon enough.

"Sometimes many days go by without our being able to leave the house," Mariam says. "When there are bombings, we have to hide. War comes to places where poor people live. We're poor, that's why we have war."

The Commander of the Faithful, the one-eyed leader of the Taliban, has extended his misogynistic dictatorship throughout most of the country, but he has been unable to quash the people of the north and minority groups such as the Hazaras and the Sadats. It is the end of the year 2000, and the rebels who are still resisting in Bamiyan have seized control of the district of Yakawlang ("the beautiful land"), where Mariam lives, though they're pitifully armed with a few shabby Soviet-era weapons. The Taliban, furious, have decided that the time has come to wipe out the flat noses of the Hazaras once and for all. The Taliban commander, Abdul Sattar, leads hundreds of soldiers in retaking the area in January 2001. He shouts, "Allah is great," burns everything in his path, and calls for the head of every single Hazara man.

Deciding who is to be executed isn't an easy task: there's an age at which it's not clear whether a boy has yet become a man. If a boy has any hair on his face, the Taliban could take him away, but if he hasn't grown much and still has boyish features, they might not see him as a threat. The same difficulties arise with old men. Life is so hard in Afghanistan that many middle-aged men look like they're approaching eighty. Yet the Afghans are such a strong, vital people that many old people are unusually active for their age. And so the process comes down to this: anyone capable of holding a weapon will die. Everything is decided in just a few seconds. The Taliban go into the houses and say, "You stand over here. You stand over there." And so on, until all the inhabitants of the village have been divided into those who will be executed and those who will watch as their loved ones are executed. Some of the men arrested in Nayak, in the middle of Yakawlang, are taken behind the Shor Aab Hospital next to the headquarters of Oxfam, an NGO. The Taliban tie their hands with their own turbans and shoot them one after another, making sure that brothers watch their brothers die, and fathers, their sons.

The Taliban scour the area around Nayak for days, searching for Hazara men and executing them, until they finally arrive at the house where Mariam lives with her parents, her aunt and uncle, and three cousins. The men, young and old alike, have had time to flee. The women have been waiting for the Taliban in their houses and tell them that all the men have died in the war. It would be a ridiculous excuse anywhere else, but not in this country of widows.

"Where are they?" the Taliban commander asks, enraged.

The women are silent.

"Where are the men?" one of the soldiers asks again, knocking one of the women to the ground with a sharp blow from his riding crop.

The soldiers start beating the women. The men hear their cries and emerge from their hiding places to surrender. Their hands are tied and they're led away, and the women wait for them to return for three days. On the fourth day, they gather blankets and a few supplies and start walking through the snow. They organize parties to search for the missing fathers, brothers, and sons, burying them as they find their corpses. Mariam, her mother, and her aunt find the bodies of three young men four kilometers from their house. They're so frozen in the ice that only a little of their clothing is visible. "We couldn't get them out, they were buried in the snow. We tried to dig them out with our hands, and we saw it was my three cousins. We wept as we uncovered them. Then we buried them again. All the women wept," Mariam remembers. She found her father beside the corpses, still alive—he'd been deemed too old to wield a weapon.

Terrified, fearing the soldiers might return at any moment, the women decide to flee Afghanistan. They want to leave fear behind, reach the Pakistan border, cross to the other side, and never again scan the sky for a monsoon that never comes and a war that never leaves. They've decided to abandon their land and escape the Bamiyan Valley.

Nobody remembers it now, but war hasn't always been the status quo in Afghanistan, even though for its inhabitants war has become an inevitable calamity like drought, earthquakes, and hard winters. In the 1960s and '70s, Kabul was a destination for European backpackers, wealthy Pakistanis headed for the Afghan capital to dance in the nightclubs, and the women wore jeans in winter and skirts in summer. But Afghanistan's fate, like that of Cambodia and so many other places, was to be decided in conference rooms thousands of kilometers away.

The Soviets invaded the country in December 1979 to support the communist government that had recently seized power in a coup d'état, forcing young Afghans to take up arms to defend their dignity, their property, and their families. The United States spotted an opportunity to undermine its Cold War rival and decided to offer the rebels weapons and training. Afghanistan became the mother of all holy wars. Fighters from all over the Muslim world—including the then-unknown Osama bin Laden—came to Afghanistan to join the war, won it, and helped topple an empire that, like all empires, needed to believe and to make others believe that it was invincible in order to survive. After the victory and the Soviet retreat, many of the foreign volunteers returned to their countries, hoping in vain to be received as heroes, more convinced than ever of the superiority of their god and forgetting that the path to victory had been made smooth for them not by Allah but by a combination of American Stinger missiles, Saudi money, and the innate human tendency to resist foreign invaders. It wasn't long before the rest of the world, with the United States at its head, forgot about Afghanistan and the people who'd liberated their land, leaving the different local factions who'd battled the Soviets to fight over what remained of the country. The Taliban and their Islamic puritanism won that civil war, bolstered by Pakistan's support and the Afghans' desire to have someone restore order to the chaos.

The Arab mujahidin, disappointed by the reception they'd gotten in their own countries and trained only in war, looked for other battlefields, from Kashmir to Mindanao, only to end up returning to the one place that welcomed them the way they believed they deserved: Afghanistan. They wanted to feel the power of weapons again, the indescribable sensation of victory against the infidels, the sweet taste of triumph. They needed a new enemy and found it in the West and in its greatest symbol, America, biting the hand that had fed their fury for so many years. And so another war began in Afghanistan. Or was it all part of the same interminable war? Osama bin Laden and his fighters now had a dream that went beyond the Afghan border: they would take the fear that grips Afghan children to the heart of the West. The Westerners would spot an airplane flying over New York, Paris, or London and think of an attack. One little Hazara girl in Afghanistan and another in the United States, their lives so different, would share for a moment the same anguish; they'd both scan the sky anxiously and, upon hearing an airplane engine, feel the same fear.

September 11, 2001. Long before I realize the world is changing before my eyes, one of my first thoughts when I see the Twin Towers fall is of Afghanistan. The next morning, I wake up to find a message from the newspaper confirming my next destination: "Get to Afghanistan as soon as you can. The Americans are going to respond there first."

While studying journalism at university, I'd wanted only to be a war correspondent. While my professors explained the five W's —the who, what, when, where, and why of journalism—in my mind I was off to somewhere in the Middle East, Africa, or Asia, imagining myself filing vivid copy from the trenches. I had no idea that the persona of the war correspondent I romanticized had been dying out for some time, a casualty of modern forms of warfare in which both warring factions are determined to hide the truth. My first few years in Asia, I'd had the opportunity to cover conflicts in Indonesia, Kashmir, the southern Philippines, and East Timor. This time would be different, because Afghanistan was *the* story. It wasn't one of those forgotten conflicts where my articles had to compete for column inches with gossip about the royal family or soccer scores. It was going to be prime time war.

I fly Pakistan International Airlines (PIA)—known as "Perhaps I'll Arrive" to those of us who have endured its perpetual delays and cancellations—to the Pakistani capital, Islamabad. In the lobby of the Marriott, the camera equipment and reporters' suitcases are starting to pile up. Anchors from some of the major television channels are reporting live in bulletproof vests from the hotel balcony. They make it all look terribly thrilling, except that the fighting hasn't started yet and, unless the Americans are execrable shots, the bullets will be whizzing by our heads more than two hundred kilometers away, in the country next door. The tourists of journalism have also arrived, special correspondents who have never covered anything more rousing than a local press conference. They are well supplied with maps and canteens and ready to describe Islamabad, the most boring city on earth, as an exciting place. Rounding out the tribe are a few good reporters prepared to risk everything in order to tell the truth; some veterans who have seen a thousand battles (with a number of great journalists sprinkled among the cocksure brats who prefer the hotel bar to the front); and finally, the most numerous group, journalists obsessed with hitting it big, with becoming more newsworthy than the news itself—not an easy task in a war zone. They dream of writing a book and narrating the next conflict in a bulletproof vest on a balcony hundreds of kilometers from the action. War, for them, is the backdrop against which they hope to become stars. The people suffering around them are the extras.

We already know how the war will begin and end, predictable as a bad movie: the Taliban have been sheltering the principal leaders of the Al Qaeda terrorist organization for years and have allowed bin Laden to set up training camps and a base from which to organize his attacks on the United States. If the Taliban don't turn over their guests—and it takes only a quick glance at how far they live from reality to be sure they won't—so many bombs are going to rain down on Afghanistan that the Russian incursions of the 1980s will look like child's play.

Every day, the tribe of journalists gathers at breakfast like children in a school cafeteria. They ask each other what they're going to do that day—*listen, amigo, what are you planning to write, what's cooking over there, where's the action today?* It's a sort of brainstorming that ensures that once anybody has a story, it gets passed from colleague to colleague until everybody's written the same thing, and the process starts over again. One of those reports involves visiting the tribal regions of Pakistan and interviewing students from the Koranic schools who, knapsacks in hand, are heading for Afghanistan "to kill Americans." Rahatullah, a young man of twenty-five who has fought in the army of the Commander of the Faithful before, claims to be waiting impatiently for the battle to begin. The reason for his optimism is simple: Americans enjoy so many of the treats of modern life—big houses, fancy cars, great fun, and all the other things he sees on those TV programs—that they'll be even more terrified of dying and losing everything than he is. For him and his friends, on the other hand, Rahatullah tells us, the good part comes after death, when they reach that paradise of virgins and milky rivers that the clerics talk about in the mosques.

"I'm going to enjoy this jihad," he says, happy as a child, the night before he is set to leave.

I spend the days leading up to Operation Enduring Freedom with stories like Rahatullah's, and the nights in the United Nations Club, one of the few places in town that serve alcohol. Though its name supposedly represents cultural diversity, it doesn't admit locals. The place is a lot Club and very little United Nations. At night, it's packed with journalists. Some nights, after the club closes, the Finnish journalist Pekka Mykkanen and I look for a place to have one last drink and end up at the China Club, where rich Pakistanis hire Russian prostitutes and drink gin before tut-tutting the next day about moral degeneracy and the deleterious influence of the West. My colleague has lost that delight in the profession that he expressed on the airplane in the Philippines after Estrada's ouster—"Isn't this job incredible? We were just in a fucking revolution"—and is fed up, ready to leave the tribe and this spectacle of a war that hasn't even started yet.

"This war coverage is a farce," says Pekka, making no effort to hide his disappointment. "Everybody just parrots what the Americans say at the press conferences, and some even make things up out of whole cloth. It's just one big ego competition."

Sunday, October 7, 2001: The spectacle begins. The first bombings target Kandahar, Kabul, and the northern front, where Taliban soldiers have been fighting for years to capture the last corner of the country controlled by the Northern Alliance. I pick up a notepad and rush out to take down reactions on the streets of Islamabad, which as war looms have been clogged with daily demonstrations against U.S. intervention. The elevator heads down to the ground floor and a few seconds later stops short. It rocks lightly to one side, and—whoomp—the lights go out. I'm trapped.

On the other side of the door, a bellhop tells me not to worry, to be patient. I recall that over the last few weeks, every time I've heard that phrase from a Pakistani, I've spent the next two days making photocopies and trying to rouse dozing bureaucrats who, behind their little windows, are dreaming they've snagged a government job—only to wake up and confirm that it's true: they'll never have to work again in their lives. I'm imagining my new beat as a horoscope writer—who would ever believe the elevator excuse?—when the bellhop, lever in hand, pries open the door and pokes his head in to ask if I'm all right. I file my article on time that day, and the next, and the next, but for some reason I still feel like I'm trapped in the elevator, powerless because I cannot cross the border and report the war from the front lines.

Every day, along with all the other journalists who've ended up stuck in Pakistan, I go to the Afghan embassy to try to persuade a group of bearded Taliban officials to give me a visa so I can be where the bombs are dropping. The Taliban organize press conferences on the embassy lawn and talk endlessly about paradise and epic victories, but not a word about visas. The long line of journalists in the embassy is proof that we, too, have betrayed their country. We'll do whatever it takes to get into Afghanistan, which we fled some time back because of political interests, refusing to judge events there on their own merits, by turns remembering and forgetting the Afghan people at our convenience, and following the narrative established by our governments, often acting as nothing more than a mouthpiece for its messages.

No one remembers it now, and some never even knew, but only a few months earlier, the Hazaras of Bamiyan, including Mariam's three cousins, were slaughtered in a vacuum, without newspapers or television channels finding the space to tell their story and, of course, without the attention of foreign governments. But the news programs announced it in big headlines when, weeks later, the Commander of the Faithful decided to finish off the job by eliminating the stone noses in the valley and bombed the two enormous Buddhas of Bamiyan. That's when everyone took notice. Newspapers and television channels around the globe discussed it for weeks; people held demonstrations in support of the monuments; then-Secretary General of the United Nations, Kofi Annan, pleaded for the Kabul government to step in; and even dictators in the Arab world criticized the attack on religious tolerance—though they themselves are all too familiar with intolerance. Is the life of a defenseless people truly worth less than two statues, however great their cultural value? Seeing us now begging for visas to enter the country, smiling pretty for the Taliban, I can't help thinking that we're too late.

Because it's so difficult to get a visa to Kabul, visiting the Afghan refugee camps in Pakistan has become a way to soothe journalistic despondency. These people who've fled from war are my only contact with the reality of what's happening in Afghanistan. It is here, in a camp near the border, that I've met Mariam. At first I see only her eyes peeking through the half-open door of a mud house;

she covers the rest of her face with her hijab and disappears in an instant when she sees I've spotted her. Her new home is a house with tiny windows that let in hardly any light, full of women weeping for men they've left behind and commiserating over their misfortunes. After the massacre in Yakawlang, the women and children fled and sought refuge in Pakistan. Mariam tells me the journey seemed interminable, weeks long, and that the survivors walked through the cold and snow, never looking back, burdened with that fear that is omnipresent in Afghanistan, hiding at night and starting again in the morning, until they reached the border near the Khyber Pass. Along the way, the weak and wounded were left behind. A local NGO picked the group up and gave them something to eat, some clean clothes, and this place to sleep.

As soon as they got to Pakistan, Mariam asked, "Are there Taliban here?"

"No," they told her. "No Taliban here."

And for the first time in her life, she put fear away. Safe now, Mariam tells me about a village in the Bamiyan Valley where it rains more bombs than water, where you can't go to school if you're a little girl, and where hiding is never a game. She tells me how her body trembled the day the Taliban entered her house and asked about the men of the family, and how happy she is that her father was old enough not to be executed but young enough to be able to make it to the border with her mother and her.

A few days before my visit to the refugee camp, I received a copy of a UNICEF study on the effects of violence on the mental health of Afghani children. It includes the results of a survey administered over the course of four years, with statistics that beggar belief, even in a country as damaged as Afghanistan. Half of the children interviewed claim to have seen someone die from a bomb, mine, or firearm. Two-thirds have lost a family member, and seven out of ten have seen mutilated bodies or heard people pleading for help.

Has Mariam seen anyone die from a bomb, mine, or firearm?

She nods.

Has she heard anyone pleading for help?

She nods.

Have they killed any of her family members?

"My three cousins were in the snow," she says, remembering how she helped dig them out. "We couldn't get them out. Everybody was looking for their children and crying. The mothers were crying, but they were all dead."

Mariam says that sometimes she wonders whether she'd be better off going away for good. Without hope, and with their future reflected in those mothers publicly beaten by the guardians of virtue, many Afghan girls decide to take their own lives. Because the Valley of the Buddhas lacks tall buildings from which to hurl themselves, they climb a mountain and leap into the void. Or they eat rat poison. The Taliban punish the parents for having allowed their daughters to commit an act that goes against Islam. They've reserved a special place for little girls in the hell they've made out of Afghanistan. "I'd rather die than go back to war," says Mariam.

According to the UNICEF report, nine out of ten children feel that life is not worth living.

The story of Mariam and how Afghan children live through the war is the last one I write before I call the newspaper to ask them to send one of my colleagues in my place. It's been almost two months, and I need a break from a conflict that I'm covering from too far away and a profession that I'm living from far too close. In wartime, among soldiers and politicians, tanks and fighter jets, battlefields and barracks, there is always a majority of people whose voices are drowned out by the roar of battle. I arrived in Afghanistan hoping to give their voices back to them. After weeks of fruitless effort, I'm overwhelmed by powerlessness.

Julio Fuentes, in Madrid, is delighted to learn that he'll be sent to replace me. He shows up in Islamabad a few days later, eyes alight and eager as a child, even though he's been in more wars than a four-star general, collecting the horrors of war as if they were stones in a backpack that grows progressively heavier and more difficult to carry. As we eat breakfast in the Marriott, I tell him what things are like here and we talk about working as a war correspondent. Things weren't always this way, he tells me.

"The media have sold out. These days they only care about money. The governments and armies have done everything they can to get rid of us, and with some frequency they succeed. They don't care about people."

I say goodbye to Julio, wishing him the same luck that has accompanied him through so many conflicts—but that on this occasion will fail him. The borders that for weeks have been closed to me open for him as soon as he lands in Islamabad, as if someone had been hiding behind the door waiting for me to leave. The Taliban regime is collapsing. Many times in the past, the Afghans have shown that they are ready to give their lives for their country, but nobody lifts a finger to save a regime that's made its people's lives miserable. Kabul has fallen, and when I hear the news the first thing that comes to mind is my encounter with Rahatullah on the border, right before he left for the front to fight in the holy war. After only a few days of bombing, thousands of Rahatullahs went running for the hills. And who could blame them: one after another, tanks, artillery, and Taliban watch posts are reduced to cinders with surgical precision. The trenches are useless when it's raining bombs that leave craters the size of a soccer field.

The mujahidin crossed the border convinced they were traveling to paradise, and they found themselves in hell. All at once, they hesitate: Will a world of virgins and milky rivers really be waiting for me if one of those bombs blows me to bits? Or will I end up outside the gates, like those amputee veterans of the war against the Soviets who beg for money on the streets of Rawalpindi, dragging themselves along the ground because they don't have the money for a prosthesis?

If it really exists, paradise can wait.

The fall of the regime turns Afghanistan into a lawless country overnight. By brutally reinstating the medieval penal code and holding public executions at soccer matches in the Kabul stadium, the students of Kandahar have managed to maintain order. Now, as the guardians of virtue retreat to their villages, mixing with the rest of the population, there's no police or army left, nobody to set the rules. There is probably no place on earth right now where life is worth less than in Afghanistan, which is threadbare with war, repression, and poverty. And in Afghanistan there are few places where life is worth less than in the Sarobi Pass, a favorite spot of highway robbers and cutthroats since the nineteenth century and a fatal ambush point for Russian tanks during the years of occupation.

Julio Fuentes, the Italian journalist Maria Grazia Cutuli, and Reuters reporters Harry Burton and Aziz Ullah Haidari enter the country by road and after a few days in Jalalabad decide to rent a car and drive through the gorge to reach Kabul. A mix of bandits and renegade Taliban stop their car midway, near the Tangi Abrishum Bridge. Aziz Ullah Haidari, the only Afghan among the four journalists, realizes it's not a simple robbery and asks for mercy— we're just journalists, we're not on anybody's side, we're just here to do our jobs. They're executed in cold blood.

The phone rings in my house in Hong Kong. People have heard that an *El Mundo* reporter has been killed in Afghanistan, and they think it was me. When they hear my voice, they sigh with relief: "Jesus, are you all right? We thought you were dead." I tell myself it's silly to think I'm at all responsible for what happened, but I can't help feeling that Julio would be alive had I not called the paper and asked for a replacement. Maybe it was my war, Julio, and not yours. Mónica is going to travel to Afghanistan to collect her husband's body, and she asks me to accompany her. In Peshawar, they're still waiting for Julio at the Pearl Continental Hotel. We tell them he won't be coming, pay his bill, and collect his belongings before meeting the truck that's bringing his body from the other side of the border. We take it to the Spanish embassy in Islamabad. That night, we reminisce about him, talking about the wars where he'd been luckier, and at dawn the two of them, Mónica and Julio, go back to Madrid together. I stay to finish Julio's work, for real this time, until the end.

"Be careful," Mónica tells me. Only two years later, she'll take up her dead husband's mantle to cover the Iraq war for the newspaper and herself become a war correspondent. "Do you hear me? It's not worth it . . . dying like that."

I've secured a spot on the United Nations plane that's flying to Afghanistan and the room that nobody wanted in the Intercontinental Hotel in Kabul. The walls are pockmarked with bullet holes, and my worktable has been cobbled together from four pieces of wood. A generator keeps my computer running during power outages. A frigid winter wind blows in through the broken windows, which shattered during a mortar attack. I write hurriedly in this icebox, desiring only to file my article and crawl into the sleeping bag I bought in Islamabad from a secondhand merchant who assured me it was the same one used by Pakistani soldiers in Kashmir. I had to haggle with him to get a good price.

"It can't be very good," I told the merchant. "I was in Kashmir last year, and an officer there told me that more than seventy percent of the casualties among his men were because of the cold."

"If you die in this sleeping bag," he teased me, "you can come and ask for your money back."

The Intercontinental has seen better days. King Zahir inaugurated the hotel in 1969, and for a few years it was the place to be for the Afghan elite, Bollywood stars, prime ministers on official visits, and tourists stopping in the city. The bellhop, Mohamed Ayan, has opened the door to all of them, touching the visor of his cap and greeting them with "Mohamed, at your service." Mohamed arrived in Kabul in the 1960s to carry out his military service, and on his first day in the city he was impressed by the traffic cops' uniforms. He decided he needed to find a job where he could wear a uniform, because that was the only way he'd be able to go through life dressed well and find a wife. Both of his wishes were fulfilled, but he never imagined that he'd live through the fall of the monarchy, the Soviet invasion, the civil war, the arrival of the Taliban, and the American bombings after the September 11th attacks, all without budging from the main entrance of the Intercontinental, dressed in his jacket and peaked cap.

"There have been periods where we haven't seen a visitor for months," Mohamed tells me. "But I come every day, just in case somebody shows up and to look after the hotel, I'm fond of it."

I've been seeing Mohamed year after year on my trips to

Afghanistan, until on one of my most recent visits I found him rather dispirited. He told me he was retiring. "What kind of country is this, where it rains more bombs than water! The hotel and I have gotten old waiting for the bombs to stop falling," he said, thinking about what might have been and wasn't, for either of them, Afghanistan and the Intercontinental.

From my room at dawn, I have an unmatched view of Kabul shrouded in morning fog. The sky is streaked with the contrails of American planes heading for the mountains of Tora Bora. The war is over in much of Afghanistan, and it's in the mountains around Jalalabad that the next-to-last battle is being fought. Tora Bora is the last Taliban holdout and the place where the United States believes it has located Osama bin Laden. The American troops are focusing all their efforts on that region, so if I want to cover the war and the possible capture of bin Laden up close, I have to get there as soon as possible. Getting to Tora Bora, though, means going through the Sarobi Pass on the same road where Julio was killed just a few days ago. Everybody's got a story about Sarobi. A week before, six Afghans were forced to get off a bus and were mutilated—their ears and noses severed—because their beards weren't long enough. A couple of days ago, a Polish reporter showed up in the Intercontinental lobby wearing only his underwear after being attacked.

Farhad, my driver, reassures me. He says he's made the trip many times and knows the trick for traveling that road without getting your throat slit.

"Never stop," he says. "No matter what happens, even if I have to run somebody over, I hit the gas. I never take my foot off the gas."

"Yes, no matter what," I repeat, as if trying to replicate his determination.

The road is made of sand and stones, full of potholes, ideal for ambushes. Cliffs crowd the road as soon as we leave the city, trapping travelers in a narrow space between the river on the left and the wall of rocks on the right. The car ahead of us kicks up a trail of dust that clouds everything around us. In many sections, vehicles are unable to travel more than ten or fifteen kilometers per hour, and the only business we've seen is a roadside stand selling AK-47s. There's nothing alive in sight: the mountains have no vegetation and hardly anybody lives in the war-ravaged villages. "Never stop," Farhad murmurs to himself every few kilometers, pressing the gas. Seven hours and one hundred forty-seven kilometers later, we arrive in Jalalabad.

We go in on renting the house of a local warlord with a few other journalists. It's not a bad place. The amenities are somewhat lacking, but that's to be expected in a country where there are a hundred guns for every telephone line and nobody under the age of thirty can remember a single day when the country wasn't at war. Every morning, one of the warlord's men bangs on the door of the room I'm sharing with Ricardo Ortega, special correspondent from Spain's Antena 3 channel. When we blearily open the door, there he is with an AK-47. He spits the only word of English he's learned—*money!*— and holds out his hand for a wad of dollars.

"Nobody gets out without paying," jokes Ricardo, who will also lose his life on the job, three years later, on the streets of Haiti.

The last bullet of a war is almost always reserved for a journalist. Some say it's for the rookie who doesn't yet know enough, others for the veteran who's convinced he knows it all. But no, that bullet is for the person who has the bad luck—and the courage—to be in the right place at the wrong time.

Every morning after we pay up, we take a taxi to the war. We head out of Jalalabad and less than two hours later we're in the mountains of Tora Bora. The last part of the trip takes us down hair-raising roads, narrow and pitted, where one careless movement would be enough to send us over a precipice. Our driver, Abdul, doesn't seem worried. He drives full speed ahead, skidding around curves as if he were on a German freeway, climbing the road to Tora Bora with music blasting from his cassette deck. Every day I want to turn off the damn music so Abdul can concentrate on the road, but I think of the five years that Afghans have spent receiving orders about what they can and cannot do, and I bite my tongue. My drives down ragged roads with fearless types like Abdul have always been more excruciating for me than the destinations themselves, no matter how awful. As soon as we arrive in Tora Bora, I am seized by a sense of absolute relaxation, as if I've just gotten off a roller coaster.

We set up on an esplanade that's been taken over by journalists. It has views of the nearby hills where the U.S. military is looking for their public enemy number one. But the Americans have never heard the local maxim: You can rent an Afghan but never buy him. They've paid the local fighters, who've never known anything but war, to do their work for them and bring them bin Laden's head on a silver platter. Osama bin Laden is familiar with the saying: the Americans don't realize it yet, but he's going to pay the mujahidin a little bit more so they'll look the other way as he slips away in one of the most infamous getaways in history.

Every day is the same in Tora Bora. The television channels set up their tripods and video cameras on the esplanade, with its remarkable view of the mountains where the combat is taking place, and the cameramen can practically lie down and take a nap. It's like watching a movie: every once in a while a B-52 appears, drops its payload in front of us, and disappears into the distance while the soldiers of Allah fire vainly in all directions. First we see the cloud of smoke thrown up by the impact of the bombs, and then, after a delay, we hear the roar of the explosion. In those stretches where there's a lull in the action, we have time to get a drink, chat with friends, and call home on a satellite phone. I get a call from my mother.

"How is everything?" she asks, worried.

"Everything's great, Mom, don't worry."

A bomb rumbles in the distance.

"So what was that, then?"

"Nothing, it was just some thunder. Looks like it's going to rain. Everything's fine. Look, I'll call you some other time."

At last, for real this time, is the spectacle of modern warfare, spread before me in all its splendor and misery.

When the bombs finally stop falling in the hills of Tora Bora, Osama bin Laden has escaped, his dreams of terrorizing the West intact. He will not be found for another ten years, when I rush to Pakistan to cover the news of his death.

A strange sense of peace settles over Afghanistan. For a time there are no bombings, no burning villages, no executions of innocents for being men enough to wield a weapon. I take the same road that Mariam and the women of Yakawlang took in their flight from Afghanistan and cross the Khyber Pass to Pakistan. I'm on my way home. Over the next few months, hundreds of trucks loaded with refugees make the same trip in reverse. They've been waiting for the war to end for decades; they long for an Afghanistan free from fear. Before going back home, I visit the camp where I first met Mariam. An old woman tells me that Mariam and her family have also left to return to Bamiyan.

"The war is over!" the woman says exultantly, unaware that the Taliban are preparing a new assault on power and that soon bombs will rain down on Afghanistan once more. Is it another war, or just part of the same neverending one?

Yeshe

If you occupy a country that isn't yours, entering your neighbor's house without knocking, and robbing him of the dignity of his home, history tells us that you can expect fierce resistance. That's what has happened over and over again with the Afghan people, the most generous hosts to their guests and the most feared enemy of their invaders. But the Tibetans are not Afghans. Their strength resides not in knowing how to answer one punch with another but in controlling the urge to return the blow. Even today, after decades of plundering and repression, their traditions violated and their children imprisoned, Tibetans are stubbornly nonviolent in their struggle against the occupation of their land.

I have been obsessed with visiting Tibet ever since arriving in Asia, in large part because of my fascination with its people, who have managed to defy with such determination the worst instincts of human nature, both in their enemies and especially in themselves. The Tibetans are prepared to lose everything except the principles that make them who they are, convinced that defeat will only come on the day when they abandon those principles and return the blow.

The first time I attempt to travel to Tibet, I try to go the official route, requesting permission as a journalist. But journalists are rarely welcome in a dictatorship, especially when they're visiting a country that's been crushed under the heel of that dictatorship. I've also chosen a touchy moment, as we're coming up on the fortieth anniversary of the Tibetan rebellion against the Chinese, the army's subsequent repression of the Tibetan people, and the Dalai Lama's flight to India. My only option, if I want to get a story in time for the anniversary, is to fly to the Chinese city of Chengdu and join one of the tourist groups authorized to enter the region.

My papers in order, I leave for Lhasa in February 1999. I'm accompanied by a flock of twenty-odd European and Asian tourists, all of us herded along by a Chinese government guide who keeps telling us, unprompted, that we're going to a place where "everything is wonderful" and happiness infinite thanks to the Communist Party. The regime has started filling Tibet with clueless guides who have never been to the region and are ignorant of its culture and history; their job is to parrot the official propaganda. Tibetans have thus lost one of the few employment possibilities they had left. All other options, from waiter to bellhop, are no longer possible as new rules require that candidates be able to speak and write Mandarin, which ensures that jobs go primarily to the Han immigrants flooding into Tibet.

They put us up in the Holiday Inn in the Tibetan capital. The American hotel chain has had a contract with the Chinese government since 1986 to run the hotels in Chinese territory, and I find promotional brochures on the nightstand that describe Tibet as "a magical world where the local people speak of their past with pride." The copy fails to mention the many Tibetans who are in jail for speaking of their past with pride, but Western businessmen don't tend to worry much about such things. Tibet has opened up to tourism, and it would be in bad taste to tell newcomers to Lhasa that a segment of the local population is wasting away in dungeons nearby.

At the hotel, we each receive a map, a nametag, and a yellow cap that we're supposed to wear at all times to visibly identify ourselves as tourists. Beside me is a woman from Hong Kong who suffers from altitude sickness and has a tube in her nose supplying her with extra doses of oxygen. She removes it only to complain about some aspect of the trip. "I paid a fortune for this, and this is what they feed us?" "Did you see how dirty the hotel carpet is?" "This is unacceptable." Our guide tells us to meet in the lobby at seven for breakfast the next day before we head out to visit "the great modernization projects that Tibet has carried out, thanks to the Party." I set my alarm clock for an hour earlier and slip out of the hotel, leaving a note at reception.

"I'm sorry," I write. "I think I've got altitude sickness. I don't feel well, so I'm taking the first flight home. Thank you for everything."

My first stop is the Potala Palace, erected at 3,700 meters above sea level on Hongshan Mountain. From the palace, you can see Lhasa in all its immaculate glory, its scars invisible from afar. Not even the most adulatory tourist brochures at the Holiday Inn could exaggerate its beauty. I am walking down one of the shadowy halls of the palace when someone comes up behind me and starts whispering words of sedition in my ear. "Don't bother leaving money in the temples. They say it's to repair the buildings, but Chinese officials keep it all." I imagine it's another tourist and keep walking, ignoring the voice. It speaks again, hardly audible. "You know, things are really bad in Tibet. The temple is full of microphones and closed-circuit cameras. They say it's to guard against thieves, but they're really there to keep an eye on us." I turn, and there in a pool of light I see a little monk with a boyish face, chubby red cheeks, gleaming pate—surely recently shaved—and the open smile of a cartoon character. He's just a kid.

"If that's true, they must be listening to what you're saying to me right now," I tell him, unaware that I, too, am now whispering.

"Maybe," the little monk answers, "but I'm not afraid. Others are, but not me."

Yeshe[1] offers to show me areas of the palace that are closed to the public and afterward invites me to tea. His room is in the attic of one of the towers of the monastery, in a section that looks like it's been abandoned. The wooden roof has large holes in it, and the little monk has grown accustomed to sharing his lodgings with all sorts of birds who wheel through the space, looking for a way out. It was true: the money from the offerings to the Buddha is clearly not being used for repairs, at least not in the monks' rooms. The cell has a rickety bed, an old rug, a trunk, a teakettle, and a small shrine for prayers. There are a few rats, but of course in a Buddhist monastery there's not much that can be done about them without breaking the rule that forbids the killing of any living being, however unpleasant. "They don't bother me, and I don't bother them," Yeshe says.

---

[1] Names and some biographical details in this chapter have been omitted or changed to protect the identity of individuals.

The walls are papered with portraits of the Dalai Lama. There are large ones and small ones, in black-and-white and in color, many of them yellowed with age. There are young Dalai Lamas, teenage ones, young men, adults, all mixed together in a large, colorful collage that reminds me of a teenager's bedroom plastered with photos of favorite rock stars. Only a few meters away, on the top floor of the White Palace, the former chambers of the Dalai Lama remain just as he left them when he went into exile four decades ago. Yeshe says that at night he can imagine the Dalai Lama there, studying in silence, and that the thought makes him feel closer to him. "I think he's not far away, and that gives me strength."

Yeshe had just turned fourteen when his family sent him to Lhasa more than six years ago. It's common for Tibetan families to dream that at least one of their sons will enter a monastery, whether in Tibetan exile in Dharamsala, India, or in some part of occupied Tibet. Norbu, Yeshe's father, chose the Tibetan capital because he was convinced that the Dalai Lama would return from exile soon.

"When he comes back, you'll be able to serve him," he told Yeshe.

Norbu offered a goat to a group of pilgrims traveling to the capital so that they'd take Yeshe with them. His son, he was convinced, was destined for something greater than raising livestock. With the help of his only neighbor who knew how to write, Norbu composed a letter explaining that Yeshe was a good boy, hardworking and studious, and that the time had come for him to "seek the path to enlightenment." Yeshe was supposed to deliver the message to the first monk he saw at the doors of the Potala Palace. If the monk had a good heart, he'd signal his permission to the Chinese authorities and help him enter the palace.

The young monk isn't sad when he thinks back on the day he left his village near Qamdo in the eastern reaches of Tibet. The neighbors came out to cheer him on his way, filling his saddlebags with food and saying their farewells with obvious envy for the boy who was going off to meet the Defender of the Faith. They would all have given anything to be in his place. His mother was sobbing, but with happiness. His three brothers, too, were envious but not bitter. His friends were proud to know him. The long journey to Lhasa, all on foot, lasted several weeks. Many times along the way, Yeshe thought he'd never reach the city or see the Dalai Lama. The supplies his family and neighbors had given him soon ran out, and for much of the trip the group had to depend on charity. When he finally arrived in Lhasa, filthy and exhausted, the aspiring monk did what his father had told him. He waited outside the Potala Palace and went up to the first monk he saw to introduce himself and deliver his letter. The monk's name was Rinzen, and from that moment he would become Yeshe's teacher and his friend.

At the time, it had already become very difficult to be admitted to a monastery. More than a hundred thousand monks had filled the monasteries in 1949, but now only a few thousand remained after nearly six thousand monasteries had been destroyed by the Chinese army, some used as targets during artillery drills. Chinese officials had set a maximum number of monks per temple, and the Potala Palace, which because of its symbolic value was more vigilantly controlled, was already over its limit. Rinzen decided to break the rules and made a nook for the boy in his own cell, teaching Yeshe about Tibet's situation under Chinese rule in long late-night conversations that could well have ended with both of them in jail. Yeshe learned from his teacher not only his dangerous habit of talking to tourists in the corridors of Potala, but also to always maintain his dignity in front of the Chinese soldiers and defend Tibetan culture. The day they came to take Rinzen away, Yeshe understood better than ever why his mentor had so often told him that Tibet was losing its fight for survival.

"He was like a second father to me," Yeshe tells me, still shaken by a recent visit to his friend in his jail cell. "He always said bad things about the Chinese to the tourists. He was sentenced to ten years for 'threatening the security of the State.' He's blind in one eye from the guards' beatings, and he can hardly walk. He's very sick. They've taken a lot of people like him away."

A few days before my arrival in Lhasa, the soldiers also visited Yeshe's room and searched his belongings. Having portraits of the Dalai Lama has been declared illegal, but the rule is inconsistently applied. Charges are more likely as sensitive dates approach. The soldiers' reactions are impossible to predict. Accompanied by two soldiers, an officer entered Yeshe's room at night and woke him with a kick in the side.

"Don't you know it's prohibited to have photos of pro-independence figures?" he asked. "Take these down immediately."

"I can't do that," Yeshe answered, trying not to seem defiant.

"What the hell are these people thinking?" the officer asked indignantly. "He's a man, just a man. Why the hell can't you see he's just a man? Take down those photos or we'll toss you in jail."

"I can't do that," Yeshe repeated.

The two soldiers started tearing down the portraits of the Dalai Lama. After stripping the walls bare, the three men left. Once they'd gone, Yeshe pulled out the pile of replacement photos of the Dalai Lama he keeps in his trunk, the ones he buys in the Lhasa black market whenever he has a little money. He knew they'd come back and tear them down again, but he'd put them on the wall over and over again if he had to. "Other people are afraid, but not me," he tells me, repeating what he'd said that day when I first met him in the halls of the Potala Palace. Now that I'm getting to know him, I'm afraid it's true.

It's hard for Chinese officials to understand how after nearly fifty years of occupation the Tibetan people can still regard the Dalai Lama with unwavering reverence. They've tried everything to break the Tibetans' unshakeable faith in their living Buddha. And everything has failed: repression, bribes, even development and modernization. Even before the arrival of the Chinese, Tibet had never been the Shangri-La idealized by the West in their dreams of lost horizons. Diseases decimated the population. Infrastructure was minimal, illiteracy rampant, and the political system feudal, with a few wealthy men exploiting the majority of the population, anything but the just, compassionate society one might expect in a Buddhist kingdom. The Communist Party of China has built roads, schools, hospitals, power plants, and even airports. The dictators in Beijing don't understand why the Tibetans aren't grateful for their offer of a more comfortable, modern life, for having taken them "from darkness into the light," as the official propaganda puts it.

How could they prefer cobbled roads to highways? Darkness to streetlights? Yesterday to tomorrow? Sure, in exchange we've stolen their freedom and weakened their faith as much as possible, but isn't that a fair price to pay for these new and better times? The Chinese regime doesn't understand that the Tibetans despise it because it eats away at their spirit every day, because it has shown them what a lack of compassion can do to a man, and because it has made them think, if only for a moment, about returning the blow. According to one legend, after the first years of mass repression and re-education in Tibet, Mao Zedong asked one of his officials how things were going up there. "They still love him," the official responded, referring to the Dalai Lama. "They still love him."

Yeshe has become the ideal guide for my trip through Tibet. After a couple of days in the capital, we've gone to see an old friend of his who has agreed to be our driver. I've asked him to take me far from the tourists and soldiers. "The first part is no problem," he says. "But the soldiers are everywhere." As we leave the city, we come across pilgrims making their way to the holy city, dressed in rags and their faces dusty. They prostrate themselves every few steps, stretching out on the ground with their arms extended and getting up again, making slow, painful progress toward Jokhang Temple. There is probably more praying in Tibet than in any other place on earth, even among the most conservative sects of Islam or the most fundamentalist strains of Christianity. Lhasa is the Tibetans' Mecca, and the faithful must make the journey at least once in their lives. Yeshe did it as a boy, but his odyssey has brought him no closer to his dream of seeing the Dalai Lama. "Will he come?" he asks me, and I have no idea what to tell him. He answers his own question: "Of course he will."

The young monk shows me the hidden road that leads to villages that don't appear on the maps. As the city recedes in the distance, we pass frozen rivers, yellowing fields of barley, and meadows that are silver with frost. Prayer flags blow endlessly in the wind, which will carry the prayers up to the Sky God, though he doesn't appear to have been paying attention to the Tibetans for a long time. They keep putting up their flags, convinced that someone must be listening; theirs is the unshakeable faith of a people who, there in the lap of the Himalayas, can touch the sky with their hands. They are so close to God—how can He not be listening?

We stop in the dusty stone villages. The story is always the same. The soldiers have already been there, searching the houses for photographs of the Dalai Lama and carrying off the young people who were too proud to keep their mouths shut. Many have disappeared without a trace, and no one expects them to return. The monks in the local temple have been replaced over and over again. The regime has never known how to deal with the Army of Compassion, which fights without weapons and which the Dalai Lama is able to lead in absentia. The red and starry flag of communist China flies over the entrance to each village. The old people weep for downtrodden Tibet. "Do you realize? Time is getting away from us," Yeshe says.

The Himalayan range, its walls rising majestically above the clouds, is the referee in a fight between heavyweight boxers. Historically, it has been in charge of separating two giants, China and India. The kingdoms of the snows, Tibet among them, felt safe for many years because of their isolation. Theirs was a world too inhospitable, solitary, and rough for those who didn't have it in their blood. When nothing and nobody had been able to stop Genghis Khan, the Himalayas did. What do you have to fear when you live where the world ends? But the world grew smaller and smaller and the lost kingdoms were found and scaled, their people conquered and rounded up by the people of the plains. The Himalayas ceased to be a refuge. In time, even countries that had managed to maintain their independence, like Nepal or Bhutan, were forced to open their doors, or sooner or later someone would come and tear them down. Tibet decided to keep its doors closed.

Would Tibet have been saved if it had opened up to the world earlier? If it had entered the community of nations, establishing regular diplomatic relationships, allowing foreigners into the country, and modernizing instead of remaining tied to an old-fashioned, theocratic system? It's hard to say. Tibet would still have been a tempting morsel of land for China for geopolitical reasons—it offers a strategic route to central Asia and extends the Chinese border to India, its natural enemy—and for its wealth of natural resources. It is also the source of Asia's water, which could one day quench the thirst of the Chinese population. But it would have been difficult for Mao to justify the occupation had Tibet not been—despite having its own religion, language, and culture—a half-finished country. The lamas believed that change meant Tibet would disappear. They didn't realize that it was just the opposite. Now change is coming much more quickly, imposed from the outside and without Tibetans' having any say in the matter. It's too late to think about what might have been: the blustering, ambitious neighbor has broken down the door.

All these changes can be not just seen but heard from Yeshe's room. The sound of the cymbals, the chanting of the sutras, and the recitation of the sacred texts at the Potala Palace mingle with the repetitive *boom, boom* coming from the JJ nightclub that opened a few meters from the temple. As Yeshe sees it, the soldiers haven't been the most dangerous thing in Tibet for a long time. The military conquest ended a while ago, and the destruction of the local culture is proceeding apace thanks to a wave of ethnic Hans emigrating from China.

The next step, which Yeshe fears will change Tibet forever, is the wave of commercialism brought by the newcomers, which threatens to conquer one of the last corners of the globe still immune to materialism, cleaving its people from the spirituality that has been their only defense against assimilation for so long. Little by little, Lhasa has been taken over by restaurants, massage parlors, karaoke bars decorated like brothels, and shops selling Tibetan souvenirs (made in Nepal). The shops are run by Chinese immigrants who have no idea what they're selling but are fearsome opponents when it comes time to haggle. Prostitution is now visible in Lhasa. Bulldozers mercilessly topple Tibetan-style buildings to make way for the white cement buildings with blue-tinted windows that grow like mushrooms in every Chinese city. Beijing has transported the runaway progress and dehumanization of its urban life to the heart of Tibet. A few young Tibetans have begun to distance themselves from their elders; they wear trendy sunglasses under their sheepskin hats and Nike T-shirts emblazoned with "Just Do It" under their robes. They've learned from their parents and grandparents that opposing Chinese domination only brings pain, and they figure they might as well get some benefit from their plundered country.

Yeshe cannot hide his sadness at the transformation of Tibet. He came to Lhasa to meditate and learn the teachings of the Buddha while he waited for the Dalai Lama's return, but the Potala Palace is no longer the paradise of learning he'd imagined. He gets up at five in the morning, studies furiously, and then plunges into endless discussions with the other monks looking for paths to enlightenment and wisdom. Since his arrival, everything he's done has been in preparation for the big moment when he'd stand before Him. Now, though, his optimism has vanished and the path is filled with shadows. The Buddhist readings are interrupted by re-education courses and patriotic study imposed by the Public Security Office. Party officials try to teach the monks to respect a communist system that's no longer in use in the rest of China; the hypocrisy of it exasperates Yeshe. At the end of each session, the police pass out forms on which the monks are to denounce the Dalai Lama and indicate any monk who is committing infractions. What really makes Yeshe's blood boil is that when the monks hand the forms back in, they're not all blank. "You can't trust anybody. Maybe the person who turned in Rinzen was another monk," he says sadly. Yeshe doesn't understand that not everybody is cut out to be a hero. Waiting for the Dalai Lama, he has left his childhood behind and become a young man, and his compassion has faltered. It's time now to continue his journey, lest everything he believes in fall to pieces before his eyes.

"My mind's made up," he tells me as we return to Lhasa after our trip through rural Tibet. "As soon as I have the money, I'll leave for Dharamsala to see the Dalai Lama."

Escape from Tibet: it's easier in summer, but Tibetans almost always attempt it in winter. When the temperatures fall below ten degrees below zero and the snow turns the roads into death traps, the Chinese soldiers posted on the border relax their guard and there's a better chance of getting to Nepal without being taken down by their guns. Once over the border, the final destination for those who have lost hope is Dharamsala, the Tibetan haven in India where refugees seek the protection of the Buddha beside the Dalai Lama. The oldest refugees say that their only fear on the journey to Dharamsala was dying without having had the chance to see him. The youngest are babies and children whose mothers have left them in the city and returned to Tibet to take care of the rest of the family, making a two-way journey to save the members of the future generations, educate them in the Tibetan tradition, and hope that someday they will be able to return to rebuild the country. Tibetans may have renounced violence, but that doesn't mean they're not ready to keep fighting. They've simply assumed that, in this battle for survival, they should be the ones to make all the sacrifices.

The Dalai Lama greets everyone who comes to Dharamsala, young and old, and listens to the stories of persecution that have beleaguered the nation he left behind. One of the refugees who arrived in Dharamsala, a monk who'd been jailed and tortured in a Chinese prison, is said to have told him once about the grave danger he'd faced during his captivity. "What danger was that?" the Dalai Lama asked. "The danger of losing my compassion for the Chinese," the monk replied.

Yeshe had left his village, leaving his family behind, to be close to the Dalai Lama. Now he'd been in Lhasa so long that he was beginning to think that his father had made a mistake and that the Chinese government would never let the Dalai Lama return. "Do you think the Chinese will let him?" he asks me again. I tell him I don't know, but that I'm sad to see how young people like him, the future of Tibet, are abandoning the country. If Tibetans kept leaving for Dharamsala while thousands of Han immigrants settled in Tibet, what future awaited Tibet? I could understand that the veneration that Yeshe felt for the Dalai Lama was strong, but not that it was stronger than the young monk's love for his people. Still, it didn't seem fair to judge his situation that way. Could I really ask someone to endure daily humiliation? The slow but inevitable erosion of his principles? The injustice of a stolen future? If he stayed, wouldn't Yeshe end up losing the compassion that the Dalai Lama demanded of him and that defined his being? Didn't he have the right to seek freedom?

When I leave, I slip a little money into Yeshe's trunk to help him on his journey to Dharamsala—or he can buy all the clandestine photos of the Dalai Lama that he likes, if he ends up deciding to stay. At dawn we climb out on one of the terraces of the Potala Palace, and Lhasa isn't there. It's disappeared in the thick morning fog. Slowly the city emerges, house by house, until with the first rays of the sun it is revealed in all its splendor. Before we say goodbye, I ask Yeshe to promise me something, and he has no choice but to agree with a smile. "Don't talk to tourists about politics, hidden microphones, and repression. You know if you keep it up, you're going to end up like Rinzen. And for what? Lots of tourists don't even care. They go home and forget about Tibet. But you stay." Of course, Yeshe is too young and too idealistic to be able to keep his word and hold his tongue. After that last meeting, I've called him a couple of times at the Potala Palace. The last time we spoke, before we lost touch for good, he was at it again.

"Don't say anything about what the two of us know. This phone is tapped," he told me. "Sometimes we can hear the government spies on the other end."

"Have you forgotten our promise?" I asked on the other end of the line.

"I didn't forget," he answered, laughing. "But you're not a tourist, are you?"

Harij takes me along the road of Tibetan exile. We cross Northwestern India to the beat of the single cassette tape of Bollywood music he's chosen to bring along for entertainment on our eleven-hour journey, dodging elephants and cows on roads that were no doubt built with them in mind. He assures me there's nobody like him behind the wheel. Unlike Masa, my intrepid taxi driver in Bangkok, Harij has never had an accident. While anywhere else in the world this would be reassuring, in India it only convinces me of the imminence of my demise, since anyone who drove like Harij could only have a clean record thanks to an exceedingly fortunate application of the law of probabilities that could be corrected around the next bend. It doesn't make much sense to wonder which side of the road you're supposed to drive on in India. You just drive where you feel like driving: right, left, and especially in the middle of the road. It also doesn't matter if the car approaching us has decided to occupy the same stretch of pavement. The usual procedure is for both cars to speed toward each other until finally, in a sort of Russian roulette on wheels, one gives in and hastily swerves aside.

"Ha," says Harij, pleased with himself for having won his last faceoff. "They always cave."

Reading in a moving vehicle has always made me carsick, but this time I bury my eyes in the book I've brought so I don't have to look at the highway or think about the law of probabilities. I'm reading the biography of the man I've come to interview: Jetsun Jamphel Ngawang Lobsang Yeshe Tenzin Gyatso (Holy Lord, Gentle Glory, Eloquence, Reincarnation of Compassion, Illustrious Defender of the Faith, Ocean of Wisdom). In one chapter, the Dalai Lama recounts an anecdote that says a lot about his character. He says that, as a boy, he liked to clamber up to one of the rooftops of the Potala Palace, extend his old telescope, and scan the horizon until he found the courtyard of the Shol state prison. The inmates, when they discovered the little monk watching them, immediately stopped what they were doing to bow down before their God-King in the distance. Those displays of blind devotion never ceased to embarrass Tenzin Gyatso, partly because they came from people who had the least to thank him for, but also because he is one of those spirits whose greatness stems precisely from not pretending to be better than anybody else.

The Dalai Lama retains the simplicity of childhood, as if he'd remained unchanged since then, refusing to garland his character with the petulancy and conventionalisms that we accumulate over the years. The people may consider him a god, but he remembers his more earthly frailties. When they venerate him in public, he comes down a step to stand beside them. When they treat him like a head of state, he jokes that it would be nice to have a state in the first place. And when his faithful bow before him, he blushes like the little boy who used to peer out from the rooftop of the Potala Palace to discover that what we are does not always coincide with what others see in us.

No, the fourteenth Dalai Lama was not born to lead, and yet fate has selected him for the most difficult responsibility imaginable: leading a nationless people, a stolen country. More than four decades have passed since the day the Dalai Lama remembers as the saddest of his life. It was the last day of March in 1959. After traveling hundreds of kilometers through the snow, hiding for more than three weeks from the Chinese troops occupying his realm, he arrived at the border and, with tears in his eyes, said goodbye to Tibet and to the men who'd risked everything to help him escape successfully. Then he hesitated. Wasn't it cowardly to forsake his people? Would it be better to stay and take up his people's yoke with them, or to be able to do more for them from a distance? Time has proven that he chose well—the world would have forgotten about Tibet long ago if the Dalai Lama hadn't kept his cause alive from exile—but it hasn't erased his doubts. It has only fed an enduring dream.

A dream of return.

Harij keeps his promise and drops me off safe and sound at the Chonor Guesthouse, down the street from Dharamsala Temple, before nightfall. The hotel has eleven rooms decorated in the traditional Tibetan style, a garden of cedar trees, and the serene calm of a Buddhist monastery. The location can't be beat, just a five-minute walk from the residence of the Dalai Lama and out of range of the cheap hotels full of European backpackers who come to the city seeking their inner selves. A few days earlier, I've received a message from the Dalai Lama's personal assistant, Tenzin Taklha, telling me that the interview I've been trying to get for months has been approved. The letter includes some advice about the meeting and says that time flies when you talk to the Reincarnation of Compassion, suggesting that I ask concrete, direct questions. Taklha doesn't want to come right out and say it: the Dalai Lama is a chatterbox. My friend and colleague Martin Regg from the *Toronto Star* has interviewed him a few days before and told him, "Forgive me, Your Holiness, but it is possible that I will have to interrupt you occasionally, as time is short and I have a lot of things I'd like to ask you." The Dalai Lama laughed and gave him permission to interrupt.

Dharamsala hasn't been a bad home for the Dalai Lama all these years. India lent the upper part of the village to the Tibetan leader and the thousands of his countrymen who followed him into exile. In a bad year, it's as if the monsoon has settled in over the city—it can rain three hundred days. Communications are terrible, and life is difficult, but nobody has ever seen this place as anything but a house on loan, a provisional refuge built to look like Tibet, the anteroom to a return that never actually arrives. Little Lhasa, as the locals call it, has changed a lot since the arrival of the first refugees. Photos of Richard Gere, the American actor who became a patron of the Tibetan cause, hang next to the portrait of the Dalai Lama in restaurants and in the bedrooms of Tibetan teenagers. There is more noise, and something resembling traffic, impossible to imagine just a few years earlier. In a little alleyway, the Memory Theater has opened, a tiny cinema furnished with a few benches and a heavy old television set. The poster announces the day's unsurprising selection: two screenings of the movie *Seven Years in Tibet*, with Brad Pitt. Also open now are a beauty salon and a few tourist bars mainly frequented by Israeli backpackers. It's the summer of 2003, the Middle East is at war, and there aren't many places where Israelis can go on vacation without someone trying to blow them up. Dharamsala is one of those places.

The city is torn: on the one hand, the need to preserve the old traditions that the exiles brought here along with the rest of their possessions; on the other, the need to modernize to avoid disappearing altogether. This dilemma, which has ensnared a good number of communities, is more urgent in the case of the Tibetans because their culture is being wiped out back home and they don't have much time: they must decide what they're leaving behind and what they're taking with them on their journey to save their nation. Some of the old people, for example, still believe that soccer should be outlawed. Like the first monks of the Buddhist kingdoms of the Himalayas, who were horrified to see the Europeans introducing soccer to the region, they see the soccer ball as the head of the Buddha. The youth, on the other hand, see that same ball as a symbol of identity, and they dream of qualifying for the Tibetan national team, which the Chinese bar from all international competitions but which from time to time is allowed to participate in demonstration matches. Identity—or the absence of it—is important to the Tibetans who were born in Dharamsala. Officially they belong neither to Tibet nor to China. They aren't Indian, either. They are citizens of a country that exists only in the imaginations of those who inhabit it, perched in a forgotten corner of the world, where the oxygen that sustains life is made of memories of a place that the young have never seen and the elderly would no longer recognize. Their identity cards read, "Nationality: Stateless."

The night before my meeting with the Dalai Lama, I've arranged to visit the medium of the Nechung Oracle. For centuries, Tibetans have depended on a monk with special powers, the only one able to contact the State Oracle and communicate advice to the Dalai Lama in times of crisis or before making major decisions. The current Nechung medium is named Ven Thupten Ngodup, a sturdy young monk who speaks some broken English and knows much more about life than his predecessors, who tended to live the monastic life much more rigidly in the real Tibet.

Ngodup is proof of how much things have changed. He welcomes me in a room of the monastery and holds out his hand to offer me his business card. *The Medium of Tibet's State Oracle*, it says, and, below his name, a Yahoo email address. Ngodup has a sense of humor and laughs when I note the contradiction between his ability to communicate with the beyond and his need to maintain communication with other mortals by more earthly means. I examine the card again. Yes, it is unquestionably the strangest business card I've ever received. Ngodup tells me that the Dalai Lama visited him a few hours before my arrival.

"Is he worried about something?" I ask him.

"Well, he tends to come when he's worried about something," he says, pleased by his close relationship with the Dalai Lama. "It's not easy to communicate with the Oracle. I have to go into a trance and it's a painful experience. It's not something I can do every day."

"I understand. And what is worrying the Dalai Lama?"

"I can't tell you that. It's confidential. Maybe you can ask him during the interview."

The Dalai Lama's home in Dharamsala has a nice view of the Kangra Valley. It's a simple place, quiet and without frills. Quite unlike the one thousand rooms of the Potala Palace. The first thing the Dalai Lama did when he settled here was to shed all the formalities that had distanced him from his people in the past. I am particularly grateful that he decided to put an end to the practice of sawing off the legs of his guests' chairs so they aren't taller than him, which would have made our meeting much more uncomfortable. The Dalai Lama receives me on his porch, takes my hand, and leads me through the gardens to the presence chamber, asking me on the way about my family, Spain, and my work, you journalists, always running around, you never stop. If something like human density exists, he has so much of it in his hunched body that it doesn't matter how big the room is, you have the sensation that his presence fills it completely. From the very start, he makes you feel like there's nobody more important than you, like there's nothing he'd rather do than listen to you, and like he's got all the time in the world to do so. I don't detect the least bit of that condescension that the politicians I've interviewed have shown, where everything they do, every gesture, every statement, is an attempt to remind you of how important they are. You can almost see them swelling up like a balloon. The Dalai Lama is a happy man. A happy refugee, really, because while any tourist today can get on a plane and show up in Lhasa, he is forbidden from going back home. His simple manner makes it possible to imagine him in a bar in Madrid, drinking beer with friends, talking about football and women.

"In my dreams I almost never think of myself as the Dalai Lama," he tells me with a mischievous smile. "I'm just another Buddhist monk. Whenever women appear in those dreams, I immediately remember that I'm a monk and have to be careful."

"Do women also approach the Dalai Lama in real life?"

"Oh, yes," he exclaims, laughing loudly. "In real life too, of course. Well, even more in real life. I think I've gotten at least ten marriage proposals from women. They've even cried as they asked me."

"Many men would envy you."

"I've told those women that it's a mistake to think that way—and, from a Buddhist perspective, a sin. I tell them they should think of me as a brother."

The Dalai Lama says he's a socialist at heart and that he used to admire Mao because he thought his ideas of equality were similar to those of Buddhism, but that in the end he found that the man—and communism—lacked the fundamental essence of his faith: compassion. The Dalai Lama says that, unlike in other places where the West has gone to wage war against tyranny, no oil has been found in Tibet, which makes him fear for his country's future. The Dalai Lama says he has no doubt that he will return to his land, if not in this life then in the next one, and that when the time comes to die, the moment to be reincarnated for the fifteenth time in the eternal light of the Tibetans, he'd like to go knowing that his people are safe, the same way a father wants to be sure that his children will be able to make it on their own.

"In Tibet we have a practice that consists of imagining death," he tells me. "I often wonder whether when the time comes I'll be able to go with courage."

The Dalai Lama doesn't say a word against China, its leaders, or those who have separated him from his people and oppressed his country. There is no rage or bitterness in his eyes when he describes his people's suffering. No longing for vengeance. I must have interviewed too many politicians, because at first I think it can't be real, that it must all be for show, a pose, a role played with a naturalness honed by long practice. But the minutes pass and my doubts fade. I am convinced, my cynicism disarmed. Life has shown him that a person's enemies are always too numerous to be able to defeat them all, so he has decided it is better to defeat the hatred that makes us create those enemies, as only thus can victory be assured. The Dalai Lama asks his people to have compassion for the Chinese soldier who enters a Tibetan's house at midnight to take away his child, compassion for the bureaucrat who orders the house's destruction, and compassion for those who tear down their sacred temples and offend their beliefs. Yeshe would not have been disappointed if he were sitting where I am now.

"I met an extraordinary monk in the Potala Palace," I tell the Dalai Lama at the end of our meeting. "He was my guide during the time I spent in Tibet. The soldiers used to go to his room in the palace in the middle of the night and ask him to take down the photographs of you, but he always refused. It was his dream to come to Dharamsala to meet you.

When he hears Yeshe's story, the Dalai Lama looks worried.

"You're not going to put his name in the paper, are you?" he asks. "It would put his life in danger."

"Yes, I know."

"All right, that's good," he says. "We have to be careful."

In a certain sense, in telling Yeshe's story like that, I faintly hoped that the Dalai Lama had had news of him. There aren't many monks in the Potala Palace now, and he'd surely have noticed if one of them had come to Dharamsala to meet him. But the Dalai Lama doesn't appear to remember him. Martin Regg, my colleague from the *Toronto Star*, was in Tibet a few months earlier and asked about him in the Potala Palace. The other monks told him that he'd left. Had he stayed in Lhasa, working as a tourist guide? Had his dream ended in a Chinese jail? Or maybe he'd made it and arrived in Dharamsala. His journey would not have been a new one but a continuation of the one he'd started years ago when he'd left his village in Qamdo as a boy. I can imagine him arriving at the Dalai Lama's residence and waiting his turn to be received in one of the daily audiences that His Holiness offers the refugees who come to Dharamsala, hungering for Him. They had both lived in the Potala Palace as children and they had both had to flee Tibet to save themselves and everything they believed in. Yeshe would tell Tenzin Gyatso that he had been in grave danger.

"What danger was that?" the Dalai Lama would ask.

And Yeshe would answer, "The danger of losing my compassion."

Eternal Beauty

Manhaisan hops up the stairs two at a time and pokes his wool hat, uneven bangs, and bright squirrel eyes out of the manhole. There's nobody in the street, nobody watching from the windows of the aging gray Soviet-era apartment buildings, nobody in the small pools of light that spill from the streetlamps onto the sidewalk. He stretches out his small arms to lift the heavy metal lid and drags it half a meter closer across the asphalt, trying not to make any noise. Soso has explained it all carefully: he should leave a gap small enough so that nobody will be able to come in without sliding back the cover. That way, if anybody comes when they're sleeping, the noise of the metal scraping on asphalt will warn them. But the gap should also be wide enough that they can escape quickly if they hear footsteps approaching. Manhaisan picks up two damp pieces of cardboard and sets up his bed on the widest pipe. He curls into a fetal position, trying not to roll off onto the wet floor, and squeezes his eyes shut, determined not to open them again until the first light of dawn illuminates their den. It's no fun being the scaredy-cat of the gang, but he can't keep himself from asking his friend Soso, as he does almost every night, if they're going to come tonight. Soso, annoyed, answers with his usual indifference: "How should I know? Do you think I know everything?"

Manhaisan means "eternal beauty"; Batmonh, "always strong"; Erdenechimeg, "precious jewel"; Saibatar, "valiant hero"; Ijilbatar, "same hero"; Ysuntai, "abundance"; and Jebe, "arrowhead." Mongolians give their children what may be the most beautiful names in the world—but only once the children are two or three years old and seem to be here to stay, once Tengri, the Mongolians' sky god, has accepted them as his own. Manhaisan doesn't remember it, but it must have been hard for his mother to contain her joy when she saw him emerge from her belly with his round, rosy cheeks. As she pushed him out into the world, fearing that evil spirits might carry him off into the world of shadows, she probably shouted insults at him the way only birthing mothers on the Mongolian steppes know how, making the spirits believe that the child was not worth stealing.

Manhaisan was born on camel skins in a yurt, the portable home of the nomads, in a nameless place in the middle of nowhere, a place where some say the Gobi Desert begins and others say it ends. His father moved the tent across the prairies according to whether they were blanketed with frost or with flowers. Seven years ago, everything was frost: winter stretched into April and the family couldn't find the oceans of green grasses that had once intoxicated the hordes of the emperor Genghis Khan as he made his way toward those nations fated to fall to his army. The horses died, food grew scarce, and there wasn't any milk for Manhaisan—or if there was milk for him, there wasn't any for his two siblings. The family gathered in the tent and decided that their only way out was to leave for the city.

But there was nothing for the Mongolian nomad in the city. Manhaisan's family set up the tent on the outskirts of Ulan Bator with other nomads who had come from every corner of Mongolia looking for opportunities. Without work, food, or aid, the situation grew worse, and in the end Manhaisan's parents packed up their belongings again and headed back to the steppes. But they did not take him with them. He had become a burden, so they left him in front of the Ministry of Social Affairs, hoping that some bureaucrat would help him, take him to an orphanage, and understand that his parents had committed an act not of cruelty but of love. That night, Manhaisan, only six years old, slept in one of the tunnels under the city for the first time.

The first person to tell me about Mongolia's underground children was the American photographer Paula Bronstein, whom I'd met during the destruction of East Timor by Indonesian troops in 1999.

One of the images Paula captured showed a boy sleeping beside a manhole, huddled at a few degrees below freezing in the middle of the night, too exhausted to reach his companions. Some children die like that: they fall asleep from alcohol, glue-sniffing, fatigue, hunger, or all of the above, and are found the next morning lifeless, frozen, in the same position. The story behind Paula's photograph crept inside me, and I knew that, as on other occasions in the past, I'd carry it in my head, pricking me like a thorn, until the day I could share it.

To my surprise, they're waiting for me in the Ulan Bator airport.

"You are lucky," a hunched, gangly youth tells me in the arrivals lounge, offering to take me to the hotel for ten dollars. "We're having very good weather this week."

It's seventeen degrees below zero, but it's been a few days since it snowed. Chinzorig is right: it's pretty good weather for the most inhospitable capital in the world. Chinzorig is fond of this old airport where flights sometimes take off days or even weeks late because of snowstorms and maintenance problems with the Mongolian Airlines planes. His parents live nearby, and whenever he goes to visit them, he strolls through the arrivals lounge, waves to his old workmates, and looks around for a customer so he can earn a few dollars. Chinzorig has an advantage over the other taxi drivers because he's worked as an air traffic controller and knows the schedules and contingencies: he has only to look at the amount of snow on the roads or calculate the wind speed to know whether a flight will land or take off that day.

One day, tired of watching government officials divvy up the flyover rights for Mongolia while workers like him took home a pitiful salary of one hundred dollars a month, he quit. He was just over twenty years old, with a job that anyone else would have envied, but in the control tower he felt like a stallion corralled in its pen.

"And what are you going to do now?" his boss asked, convinced that only a crazy person would give up the security of a steady paycheck in such a broken country.

"Lots of things," said Chinzorig.

The first of those things was to buy a used car with the money he'd saved and start working as a taxi driver and tourist guide.

Chinzorig offers to take me to the underground children. "During the day, they work in the train station," he says. When we get there, dozens of little porters are awaiting the arrival of the train beside the tracks, eager to transport the luggage of the disembarking passengers on their improvised wooden carts. The tallest have an advantage because, stretching their necks above the crowd, they can see who is getting out of the cars first. The smallest are able to dart among the others with their little carts. Everyone wants to get to the foreign tourists first. It's said they come from places where there is no cold, winter, or snow, places where people live in large houses and drive six-wheeled cars and, of course, have so much money that a dollar tip is no skin off their backs.

The Trans-Mongolian is coming in from Moscow this morning before heading on to Beijing, leaving the Gobi behind and winding through the mountains, valleys, and deserts that Genghis Khan traveled in 1214 on his way to the gates of what was then Zhongdu. The Mongolian wolf met no resistance at the time because the Chinese emperor Xuanzong, who had heard tales of the ferocity of the khan's warriors, appeased the visitors with carts full of treasure and a beautiful princess accompanied by five hundred servants who joined the invader's manacled army. The khan showed his gratitude by coming back three years later and destroying Zhongdu anyway. One of the witnesses to the fall of the city of Bukhara summed it up best, describing the way Genghis Khan and his men understood war in a single sentence: "They came, they sapped, they burned, they slew, they plundered, and they departed."

The Mongolian warriors, under the orders of the Oceanic Emperor and later those of his descendants, conquered everything in their path in the thirteenth century, sacking and subjugating peoples from the Black Sea to the Pacific Ocean, raising the largest land empire that man has ever known, and leaving in their wake a wave of destruction and death that would not be replicated until the Second World War. The Emperor of the Steppes, who had once declared that one of the great pleasures of life was "to scatter your enemy, to drive him before you, to see his cities reduced to ashes, to see those who love him shrouded in tears, and to gather into your bosom his wives and daughters," did not live to see the destruction of what he'd created. He would have been humiliated to witness how over the years Mongolian women would be the ones to be clasped against the chests of, first, Chinese invaders, later Russians, and today anyone with five dollars in his pocket. The young women on the dance floor at the Ulan Bator Hotel save up their money so that two or three times a year they can make the same journey that Genghis Khan did to Zhongdu. They board the Trans-Mongolian, leaving the Gobi behind, and wind through the mountains, valleys, and deserts until they arrive at Maggie's, a small pub next to the Workers Stadium in Beijing. There you can see them dancing and approaching customers drinking at the bar to whisper in their ear that a piece of the legend of Mongolia is for rent tonight.

On freezing Ulan Bator nights, when Chinzorig takes me to the nightclub at the Ulan Bator Hotel so I can see the "most beautiful women on earth," Mongolia seems to me like a man sitting alone in the corner of a bar, longing for a past that will never return and signaling for another round so he can forget about the present, which gets more painful with every sip. The melancholy of the Mongolian people is palpable in every one of the bars we visit, in the Genghis Khan Hotel, in the bottles of Genghis Khan vodka plastered with a portrait of the emperor, in the packs of Genghis Khan cigarettes, in the money printed with the face of Genghis Khan, and in Ulan Bator's wide Genghis Khan Avenue, which we fly down at top speed. Mongolians, drunk with nostalgia, live in hope that the legend will become reality, that Genghis Khan will reappear, reincarnated in a little boy born on camel skins, a boy like Manhaisan, perhaps, who will be charged with returning this land to the splendor of days gone by.

Manhaisan and Soso have earned a little money from the travelers on the Trans-Mongolian and are walking along carrying two large bags of trash when we find them near the train station entrance. Manhaisan's expression is sad, almost pained. I will later discover that it has become fixed on his face, now an intrinsic part of his physical features. Soso looks proudly ahead, more relaxed. The boys' cheeks are flushed with cold, their clothes are ragged, and as they walk they look around with wary eyes. Chinzorig speaks to them, offers them some food, and asks where they live.

"There," says Soso, pointing to the ground.

They agree to take us to their shelter.

It's not a large chamber, some fifty meters square and two meters high. The floor is half a meter deep in water, and a wave of heat smacks us when we enter. On the coldest days, you can go from thirty degrees below zero in the street to thirty degrees in the warrens beneath it, where the humidity makes the atmosphere even more suffocating. The rooms are not connected to each other and are not part of the sewer system but of the heating system installed under the city by the Soviets. The pipes, which are wide enough for the children to sleep on top of them without falling off, are connected to coal plants. The spaces where the children sleep, which vary in size and depth, were designed for maintenance access. Many of the pipes, which are full of boiling water, are starting to show their age, and occasionally one bursts. Then someone shouts, "Get out! Get out!" and they all flee the scalding flood. When any of the children die and the NGOs protest, the police organize a massive raid, round up a few hundred children, and lock them up in an old military barracks on the outskirts of Ulan Bator, where they are often humiliated and beaten before being put out on the streets again. Manhaisan and the others have learned to fear the raids.

"Are they going to come tonight?"

The group has carved their names into the walls of the chamber: the territory is marked, warning other children that this shelter is taken. Some clothes on hangers dangle from one pipe, and on an improvised shelf—a hole in the wall—there's a sliver of soap and a bottle of cologne that the older children use with all the extravagance of an eyedropper. The tunnel has two openings to the outside, one in the sidewalk and the other right in the middle of the street, so that if a child isn't careful when peeking out, the prime minister's motorcade of fabulous luxury cars could pass by at just that moment and take the child's head with it. And no one could accuse the prime minister of forgetfulness: Mongolian politicians, anxious to take advantage of the recent arrival of capitalism to get as rich as they can, don't yet appear to have noticed that four thousand Mongolian children are living underground.

Manhaisan's gang is made up of five boys and a girl. Manhaisan and Soso are the middle children. They are thirteen and fourteen years old. Batmonh, a tiny ten-year-old boy, is the youngest. Erdenechimeg, eleven, is a wild, shy girl who crawls along the pipes with the agility of a squirrel and has beautiful night-dark eyes that are always hidden under her tangled hair. She never speaks, maybe because she doesn't think there's anything interesting to say to this stranger who's entered her home without asking. Saibatar, seventeen, and his pal Ijilbatar, sixteen, are the veterans. None of them look their age: the years in the bowels of the city and the lack of food have stunted their growth, so they look two or three years younger.

The two eldest boys have gone with Batmonh to the black market, where they work as a team trying to steal wallets from tourists and absentminded locals. Chinzorig is amused—until we go to the market to watch them work and another gang ends up stealing his wallet.

"These kids are good," he says, happy that I, at least, have come out of it with my wallet intact.

The gangs of underground children share the work, and all the money they earn is portioned out to buy food, clothing, or vodka. The girls sell their bodies for five dollars at bus stops; the boys look for odd jobs and a bite to eat along the rails or, if no customers arrive on the Trans-Mongolian, sell themselves to one of the city's drunks, who almost always stumble off without paying. Life isn't easy for anybody on the streets of Ulan Bator, but it's even harder for the young people who live beneath them. Nobody asks Erdenechimeg where she gets her money.

They all know.

The first chill of winter is especially hard: that's when the great brawl for the best places to sleep breaks out. A group of older children has driven Manhaisan and his friends out of the larger, better-located tunnel where they lived in October. At the end of March, the underground realm is clearly divided into territories after brutal clashes fought with fists and knives. Venturing into foreign territory can mean a good beating, or even death. Saibatar has participated in a lot of these skirmishes and is respected among the gangs. He spent his first day on the streets in 1990, soon after the fall of the Soviets and the arrival of democracy in Mongolia. Moscow had propped up the country with $900 million in subsidies a year, supplying its people with all their assets—including their ideology—over seven decades of rule. The average Mongolian, who under the Soviets had been guaranteed a job, an apartment, food, and a pension, was forced to seek a living as the overnight arrival of capitalism threw the country into turmoil. People lost their government jobs, thousands were evicted from public housing, and the subsidies from Moscow, which had made up a third of the national economy, disappeared. The Trans-Mongolian no longer pulled into town full of Soviet officials, agriculture and industry collapsed, and society split apart at its root, the family. The first children began to be abandoned or fled families shattered by poverty, alcohol, and violence.

Saibatar's family, nomads from the Dornogov region, lost everything and decided to abandon one of their four children so they could feed the rest. They got on a train, and when it pulled in to Ulan Bator station, they gave Saibatar a bag of food, a hat, and a coat and told him to wait for them to come back. He was seven years old. For two years he lived in the same train car that had brought him to the city, making the trip home and back again over and over and waiting on the platforms for someone to come looking for him. He survived on food given to him by railroad employees until one day, on the platform in Ulan Bator, the other children asked him who he was waiting for.

"My father," Saibatar said.

"He's not coming," they told him.

He joined one of the gangs. He's been with them ever since.

As he tells his story, Saibatar tries not to cry in front of the others. He is respected and sometimes feared, the Prince of the Underground; he cannot show any weakness. Mongolian males are taught from the cradle not to display emotions, not even with their friends and family. A Mongolian man does not cry. Ever.

Saibatar has a girlfriend now. Ysuntai is a girl from the streets, fourteen years old, who sells her body at the bus station like all the others. That's where she and Saibatar met. On the coldest days of winter, the two go into the chamber, undress, and make love on the hot pipes, trying not to fall into the water pooled on the floor, huddling at the rear of the shelter where the light from the street doesn't reach. They "got married" two months ago, imitating the ceremonies that take place every day at the Wedding Palace near Nairamdal Park. Lit by a dozen candles, Saibatar told Ysuntai that they'll be together forever. The two of them have contracted syphilis, and they ask me to buy them some medicine in a pharmacy. When I return with a little penicillin, the only thing I've been able to find, Saibatar blushes and insists that he doesn't sell his body, that the disease is Ysuntai's fault. She nods her head. The Prince, down here in the tunnels, has a reputation to protect.

Sitting on one of the pipes, Manhaisan, Soso, Saibatar, and the other children tell me what life is like underground. It's not just a refuge but a parallel world. Life down here has rules, which the children know well. Some of the rules are good and some bad, but in many cases they're better than the ones that govern the streets above. It's a world of loyalty to the gang, their only family; of sharing what little they have and helping each other in order to survive; and of solidarity with the others. These are principles that the world of adults seems to have forgotten but without which it would be impossible to survive below. The street children of Ulan Bator could have been like so many others in Brazil, South Africa, or the Philippines, but the cold made them different. Their survival instinct brought them underground, and here, away from adults, they've built their own society. Those who live above them have forgotten they exist, and they prefer it that way.

One Mongolian legend describes three worlds: the sky, whose kingdoms are ruled by Tengri, the Immortal Blue Sky; the middle world, the world of humans; and the subterranean world, where the spirits dwell. The children have made the third world their home, changing their nests every season. They live on what the earth gives them—in their case, mostly trash—fighting for territory and conquering the weaker groups.

"We are the nomads of the underground. Nomads like Genghis Khan," says Saibatar.

"Yes, nomads," Ijilbatar repeats, laughing.

Manhaisan and the others are sleeping, and even though the lid of the chamber has been left as Soso instructed, neither very open nor very closed, none of the children have noticed that somebody's here. The underground children can expect four types of visits. Of these, only one can be considered good news: a visit from Father Gilbert. Religion returned to Mongolia relatively recently, after the fall of the Soviet regime. The Russians had demolished most of the Buddhist temples and in their place built monotonous apartment buildings, factories, and Communist Party offices. Thousands of monks were driven from their monasteries and forced to lead a secular life, which included wearing Western-style pants. In a single political purge in 1936, seventeen thousand lamas were executed. For Buddhism, one of Asia's major spiritual forces, that massacre was only the beginning of a century in which communist repression in Chinese-occupied Tibet and in Soviet Mongolia would carry death to the temples of compassion.

The arrival of democracy meant a reprieve. The monks who had survived were allowed to return to those temples still standing, though only to discover that they would have competition in their efforts to recapture their people's faith. Close on the heels of the fall of the communists came dozens of Christian missions ready to fill the faith vacuum. The streets of Ulan Bator filled with Western missionaries—Mormons, Seventh-day Adventists, and Southern Baptists—all hoping to introduce the Mongolians to God, who could guide them in this time of tribulation. The Vatican immediately re-established diplomatic relations with Mongolia and sent a number of missionaries. Father Gilbert was one of the priests chosen to join the Congregation of the Immaculate Heart of Mary mission.

No sooner had he arrived at his new destination than the young priest distanced himself from his colleagues' efforts to convert the population and turn the country's religious rebirth into a competition between Buddhists and Christians. Father Gilbert was made of other stuff: he was part of that new generation of missionaries who deemphasized—and sometimes neglected altogether—evangelization and instead put their energy into more earthly work. When he arrived from the tropics in 1993, the priest's primary objective had been to help the people of Ulan Bator. Only when asked did he explain which God had given him the strength to devote himself to such a task. Instead of spending the money that came in from Rome throwing parties and holding meetings with other religious groups to discuss how to attract new faithful to the flock, the priest began building a children's shelter in the Bayangol district, near the train tracks. Over the years, Father Gilbert's home became a fortress of hope in the middle of a depressed city, the only safe haven for the children of Ulan Bator.

Every Wednesday, the priest says, "Let's go," gets in his van, and ventures from manhole to manhole with hot tea and cookies. He offers shelter to those who want it and asks the children if they hurt anywhere, body or soul, as he has medicine for both maladies. His Verbist Care Center has clean beds, hot water, and a group of volunteers who try to make the children feel at home, if only for a little while. The problem for Manhaisan is that his home is underground. Father Gilbert believes that children who have been on the street longer than a year are difficult to reintegrate into society. He focuses his efforts on the younger children and the ones who have ended up on the streets most recently. "They come here and they destroy everything; they're totally feral," he complains affectionately whenever the wildest of them pull some mischief in the children's home. Manhaisan remembers having been in Father Gilbert's shelter, but he escaped through a window, unable to follow rules, sleep between white sheets, and eat with utensils. In a way, he's a bit like Mowgli, the young boy raised by wolves in the Indian jungles in Kipling's *The Jungle Book*. And yet how he would have wished for it to be the Filipino priest, who is living proof that there are countries where winter does not exist, banging on the manhole cover in the middle of the night.

But today's not Wednesday.

If it's not the day for pastries and hot tea, then it could only be one of the other three kinds of visits that the children receive underground.

None of the three is welcome. One of the rival groups could be looking for a fight, but the children's burrow is small and it's unlikely that a larger group would have it in its sights, as winter is ending. It could also be one of the gangs of wealthy youths, many of them the scions of government officials and well-connected businessmen, who from time to time come out to amuse themselves by beating up the street children. "Sometimes I dream that they seal up the manholes and we're trapped down here forever," says Manhaisan. "I'm scared of them." The third and most frightening possibility is a visit from the police. I never hear the children complain about the rats with which they share their shelter, the filth, or the damp. They talk about darkness, hunger, and especially fear—and of all their fears, the police are by far the worst.

The officer shouts down through the hole and orders the children to come out. One by one, the members of the gang are deposited in the police wagon. It's raid night, and a few dozen ragged children have been rounded up. The police generally hold them in cells at the station all night, and anything could happen between now and daybreak. Usually they're beaten, stripped, and humiliated before being released with a warning not to show their faces again anytime soon. But sometimes the beatings are so severe that the children can't go back to their maintenance vaults for weeks. Some of them disappear for good. The girls are systematically raped and return to their holes in shame, like on those days when the bus station customers refuse to pay. After the raids, the girls have to buy their freedom again, and when they return to the shelter, nobody asks them how they were released.

They all know.

These "cleaning operations" happen two or three times a year. Bruised and humiliated after their night in jail, the children return to the underground and forget their suffering by indulging in alcohol and sniffing glue, as if it were a holiday or the new year. One by one, the members of Manhaisan's gang pass the pot of glue around, put it to their noses, and inhale deeply, closing their eyes and furrowing their brows. At first it feels like a worm has crawled inside their skulls; it throws their heads into disarray, scratches the walls, and eats away at their brains. "Camel shit, camel shit!" shouts Saibatar, and they all laugh and leap in the puddled water. A shot of vodka makes the worm disappear, and the head melts, becomes a soft, velvety cloud. Then Soso, Saibatar, Ijilbatar, Batmonh, and Erdenechimeg are able to leave sad Ulan Bator, soar toward the steppes, laugh, cry, and hallucinate. They can mask their lives with other, better lives. Eventually they pass out and dream about the singers and actresses whose photos, sliced from magazines they find in the trash, decorate the walls of their underground chamber, proof that there is also life under the streets of Ulan Bator, in the Mongolian third world.

The only one who is unable to leave for a better world during these binges is Manhaisan. He's always been a frightened boy, timid and introverted. It's often difficult to get him to talk, and he sometimes suddenly, without anyone's asking him, expresses a heartrending wish—"I don't want to be scared anymore"—that brings you a little closer to the reality of his life in the sub-city. Of all the children, Manhaisan is the one who has been least able to adjust to life underground. He doesn't know how to hide his bitterness. He's not ashamed to cry—he does it all the time—not ashamed to complain when his stomach is empty or to admit that he misses his mother, whom he remembers telling him stories about camels and wild dogs in the family yurt. The others have adapted, but every moment of this life is painful for Manhaisan. His face blackened with dirt and his hands battered, he sits down on a pipe apart from the others and sobs again.

"The children who live in houses want to kill us. They say that one day they're going to close off the maintenance vaults and we'll be trapped forever," he says, returning to his worst nightmare.

"What children?"

"The ones who live in the buildings. They come and insult us, beat us with sticks, and throw things down into the hole."

"And when they come, how do you defend yourselves?"

"We don't do anything. We let them hit us."

"Why?"

"Because they live up there and we live down here."

Not four seasons but two. Warm. Cold.

The pale colors of the Gobi, a million square kilometers of solitude in the heart of Asia, turn purple with the play of light and shadows on a late summer afternoon, as if Tengri, the Immortal Blue Sky, were toying with the pale hues of the desert. As the land thaws, the steppes reveal the hidden green of their prairies, and the city, stripped of the melancholy of winter, doesn't seem quite so gray anymore. You travel to a country during the cold season, and when you return with the warmth, you no longer recognize it. It is transformed.

With the arrival of summer, the children emerge from their dens. All at once, everything seems easier in Ulan Bator. Any place—a park or a vacant lot—is a good place for sleeping. More tourists arrive at the train station, and it's easier to earn a little money carrying their luggage. For a few months, Manhaisan and the other children leave the underground world of the spirits. But come October, when freezing temperatures return, the children battle for the best chambers again, the Gobi is painted once more with stark desert colors, and many people stay home to follow the romance between the poor newspaper seller Estrellita Montenegro and the millionaire Miguel Ángel González in *Cara Sucia*, the Venezuelan soap opera that's broadcast on Mongolian television every day, with a special five-hour block on Saturdays. Mongolians watch the show without dubbing because there's no money for translating the hundreds of episodes; they follow it as if Spanish were their native language. They are learning Spanish without being aware of it, and many, believing that Estrellita and I must be from the same country, greet me by repeating her name or imitating her melodramatic gestures. And so I can enter a restaurant, greet the patrons with the local *Sain bainuu?* and hear in response something like, "*¿Por qué no me amas?* [Why don't you love me?]"

In restaurants, in homes, in public buildings, and of course at the train station, everyone feels Estrellita's misfortunes as if they were his own. Travelers waiting for a train stand transfixed by the show, which plays on the televisions in the waiting room. The children, who watch whenever they can get away with it, laugh uproariously at the love scenes. Even out on the steppes, people weep over the joys and hardships of the newspaper seller. Television has become one of the symbols of the brutal change that the nomads have experienced since the Soviets arrived in 1924, and more so since they left. The men of the prairie, vestiges of the oldest nomadic society on earth, can now travel to California beaches, watch the World Cup, and attend Victoria's Secret runway shows thanks to televisions connected to enormous satellite dishes powered by solar panels, which are themselves connected to old car batteries.

And all of it in the middle of the Gobi Desert.

When Mongolians turn on the television, they see not the progress of the United States or Europe but evidence that they themselves are falling behind. The screen shows a world of abundance suggesting that the best pastures lie in the city, where you can get fermented mare's milk just by crossing the street and entering a store. The nomads wonder whether their way of life, the Genghis Khan model, still makes any sense. Their lives have always been tied to the earth, the yurt, and the animals, but especially to the absence of fences or barbed wire, because nomads need space and the freedom to move around looking for better pastures and a more benign Tengri. Mongolians did have one thing in common with their Soviet colonizers: neither believed in private property.

Television changes Mongolians' perception of their own happiness. Their desires, needs, and ambitions are transformed. The teenage girls want pale skin, shiny hair, and a wasp waist. They ask their parents for shampoo and mud masks for their skin. They cry because they can't be like the girls on television. The young men no longer aspire to take care of animals and ride the steppes; they have no desire to walk in their fathers' footsteps. They'd rather have a job in the city. Television has awakened in them dreams that are new and unfamiliar. And sometimes false.

For the new generations of city-educated politicians, the nomadic life is a backward one. They want to parcel out the land in small private tracts to increase competition and develop small, industrialized cities where now only livestock graze. Urbanization, consumerism, and the growing wealth disparity have marginalized the nomads.

The Mongolian landscape has changed so much that people now race across the steppes on noisy Russian-built Planeta motorcycles instead of the horses on which their ancestors conquered the world. The exodus of the youth has begun. Leaving one of the trendy Ulan Bator nightclubs, I come across a scene from the American Old West: a group of teenagers have tied their horses to the trees outside the club while they gyrate to American rap on the dance floor. They've ridden hundreds of kilometers, leaving behind the yurts where they live with their parents, to spend the weekend in the capital.

Chinzorig tells me that we have to travel outside of Ulan Bator to see the changes that are upending Mongolians' lives. My air traffic controller, taxi driver, and tour guide has always dreamed of saving up enough money to buy an all-terrain vehicle and take tourists to see "the majestic mountains of Khentei, Khangai, and Soyon; the sacred rivers of Kherlen, Onon, and Tuul; the blue lakes of Khuysgul, Uvs, and Buir; the great Gobi and the sand oceans of the south," and the steppes that the Mongol poet Natsagdorj saw covered with crystal and glass in winter and with a carpet of flowers in summer. It would still be two years before the "beginning of lots of things" for Chinzorig, which would eventually lead to that all-terrain vehicle and a tour company, Golden Square, whose mission was to reveal the beauty of Mongolia to nonbelievers like me. All Mongolians are nomads at heart, and Chinzorig, though he's one of the most urban Mongolians I've met, enjoys living in yurts in the middle of nowhere, traveling across the Gobi, engaging with the people of the countryside, and showing the best of his country to people not lucky enough to know it yet. Chinzorig speaks perfect English, has travel experience, and is ready for anything. I ask him if he doesn't want to get out of here. Doesn't he want to leave for a country with more opportunities?

"Leave?" he asks, "Leave the best place on earth, with the most beautiful women and the most loyal friends? Every time I leave, I feel a yearning that pulls me back again. I don't know how to live anywhere else. Believe me, though it doesn't always seem it, Mongolia is the best place on earth."

We drive north across the prairies, and every few kilometers Chinzorig asks me what I think, whether in the places I've been in Europe, Asia, or America I've ever seen anything more beautiful than these snowy valleys, the wild horses galloping across the steppes and the vast plains turned to mirrors of ice, mirrors into which these people proudly gaze. Mongolia is no longer the man sitting alone in the corner of a bar trying to forget, but the dazzling singer who lights up the night, dressed to the nines, with her hair loose and a friendly smile that invites you to sing along. Yes, Chinzorig is right, Mongolia is a beautiful country. Truly beautiful.

In the distance, on the slope of a hill, we see a yurt and decide to stop. In it live a young couple and their five-year-old son, Jebe. Just like Manhaisan's parents years ago, they are desperately looking for a place to pasture their animals, and they've ended up less than a hundred kilometers from Ulan Bator, dangerously close to a life that isn't theirs and a place that has nothing to offer them. The year before, Mongolia suffered a severe drought, followed by harsh frosts and a winter with temperatures forty degrees below zero and icy winds. The Mongolians call this phenomenon the *dzud*, storms that ravage the grasses, starve the animals, and make life miserable for even the toughest nomads. It is the magic of the seasons in its most brutal form, when it shatters dreams. The *dzud* turns the plains of Mongolia into an immense cemetery littered with the lifeless bodies of thousands of animals, frozen solid, in a scene likely resembling the one encountered by the first travelers to Zhongdu after the city had been laid waste by Genghis Khan. It is said that, as he approached the city, one visitor wondered about a white mountain visible in the distance. The locals told him it was the bones of Zhongdu's residents, piled up by the warriors of the great khan.

In defense against the gelid monsoon, some families pile up dead animals around their tents, building a wall of carcasses to protect themselves from the bitter winds that lower the temperature another twenty degrees. The *dzud* usually pummels the steppes once every five or six years, but the new century has brought two years of *dzud* in a row and, though the Mongolians don't know it yet, two more await them still. Their animals dead, afraid their children will not survive, thousands of nomads are crowding into the outskirts of Ulan Bator in their yurts. The men, jobless and unable to adapt to their new lives, turn to drink to defeat their depression, joining the ranks of drunks who have made Ulan Bator the city with the most alcoholics per capita in the world. Some end up taking their own life, a life they no longer recognize. Every day, another child joins the dark world of the maintenance vaults underground.

The young nomad couple invites us to have some tea. The tent's entrance faces south, as tradition dictates; it is made of felt and round like the sun. To the left is a place reserved for guests and at the rear is the khoimor, where valuables are stored and the elders sit. There is also a small altar, a stove in the center, and photographs on the walls. Beside the yurt is a satellite dish connected to an old television that picks up international channels. Gounkhu, the husband, talks about the hardships of winter and asks us about life in the city. "It's hard," Chinzorig says, without mentioning that as we left Ulan Bator, we saw hundreds of yurts packed together in the barren wastes. We head back, uncertain which direction—the city or the steppes—the young family will choose. I prefer to think that they'll turn back. They almost certainly won't. Will Jebe end up living underground like Manhaisan, longing for the days when he ran free over the white-encrusted steppes of the cold season and the oceans of flower-speckled green of the hot season?

Back in Ulan Bator after our outing across the steppes, Chinzorig picks me up at the hotel and we go out to look for Manhaisan and his gang. They're not home. We go back later, but they don't return to sleep that night, even though it's snowed in Ulan Bator and the temperature has dropped again.

"They'll be here tomorrow," Chinzorig says.

We don't find them the next day, either. For two days we look for them in the streets, in the train station, in the black market, and downtown. We ask the other underground children about the gang. Nothing. I remember the last day I spent with them, when a group of locals, who'd never offered them a piece of bread or a cup of warm milk, insulted them upon seeing them with a foreigner. "Don't talk to him. You're an embarrassment to Mongolia. What will people think?" said a woman carrying grocery bags. "Somebody should call the police," said another man. That afternoon we filled the chamber with food and Coca-Cola, and for the first time I saw Manhaisan smile.

It's time for me to leave, and I'm sorry not to have seen the children at least one more time. Chinzorig calls his old workmates from the airport control tower and asks them when my flight will be taking off. It's snowing in Ulan Bator and we've got hours yet. On our way to the airport, we stop one last time at the home of the children of Genghis, in the third Mongolian world, two stories below the Immortal Blue Sky. There's nobody on the street, nobody watching from the windows of the aging gray Soviet-era apartment buildings at the end of the block—and nobody in the maintenance chamber. The entrances have been sealed. Maybe they came back, heard footsteps, and slipped stealthily through the gap that Manhaisan had left neither too open nor too closed, fleeing from the children of wealthy families or another police raid. Or maybe they decided to leave for another place—nomads of the underground, after all.

Kim

Light. Darkness.

A satellite image of the Korean Peninsula at night. The south is lit up like a Christmas tree, covered with gleaming dots. They are offices, karaoke clubs, living rooms, highways, illuminated streets, families around the television set. Light.

North of the thirty-eighth parallel, nothing. An enormous dark room. Its inhabitants inside it. Darkness.

Traveling to Darkness isn't easy. Its guardians are reluctant to open the door, lest a crack of light sneak in. The country is sealed off. In the consulate in Hong Kong, they give me a sheet of paper that says that entry is especially forbidden to "Japanese, Americans, and journalists."

"Are you any of those things?" they ask me.

"Well, uh, no, of course not."

Given that my destination is a country of lies, officially presided over by a man who died years ago and with a government that claims to have created a paradise while its people die of starvation, I imagine the vigilantes of journalistic ethics will forgive me if I become part of that lie for a few days. To get a visa, I have to show that I'm somebody I'm not. Peter Pang, the owner of the ever-efficient printers I use in Hong Kong, prepares business cards that declare me sales manager at a paper factory; a good friend writes me a letter confirming that I work for his company; and I dream up a new life for myself in the résumé requested by the consulate. I appear before the North Korean officials again with the face of a befuddled tourist, though I'm not really sure what kind of face that is. They examine my papers and verify the information I've provided. They call my friend's company, and he tells them, "Yes, Mr. Jiménez works here. He's a sales manager in paper distribution." Darkness gives me a seven-day visa.

I fly to Beijing and, from there, take an Air Koryo plane to the capital, Pyongyang. The plane takes off on a winter day in 2002, but when I land in North Korea, I am informed that I will have to adjust to a new schedule. It is the year 92. A few years back, the government decided to reset its official calendar to begin with the birth of the "eternal president," Kim Il-sung, who's been dead for eight years, though people still talk about him as if he were alive. The Sun, after all, is eternal and never stops shining. When Kim the elder left the North Koreans orphaned, the country convulsed in one of the most surreal displays of collective hysteria in history. Millions of people wept in the streets as if they'd lost the most beloved of their loved ones, in a massive competition to show the most pain possible at their leader's departure. Thousands swooned or supposedly attempted suicide. Young teenagers shook and writhed on the ground in what looked like epileptic fits. The newscaster on KCTV, the official channel of the regime, was unable to announce the death; viewers heard only his wailing and, amid howls and sobs, a few disjointed sentences. "Is it true? You've left without taking us with you? Is such pain even possible?" Since that day, North Korea has been collaboratively headed by the deceased and embalmed leader, who has retained the title of Great Leader, and by his son, Kim Jong-il, who has chosen the title of Dear Leader for himself.

Together, father and son have brought the country to ruin.

"Welcome to a place like none other," say Mr. Park and Miss Sim[1], as if they've read my thoughts, when they meet me at the airport. He is a middle-aged retired soldier and she is a young former dancer whose career was cut short by an injury. The two of them are official government guides, part of the army of spies meant to control the few foreigners who come to the most surreal and despotic dictatorship in the world. The choice of two spies is not random:

---

[1] Names and some biographical details in this chapter have been omitted or changed to protect the identity of individuals.

they are both charged with the additional mission of spying on each other and reporting back to their superiors. Rounding out the airport welcoming committee is another Mr. Park, this one behind the wheel of a black Mercedes that the government has reserved for me. The coincidence in the names of the two Mr. Parks is not as surprising as it might seem. Nearly half of the Korean population, in both north and south, share only three last names: Kim, Lee, and Park. Confucians believe that two people with the same last name are part of the same family, even if they don't know each other and the family ties date back centuries. Marriage between two people with the same last name is therefore prohibited, which is a problem, since someone named Lee has to discard hundreds of thousands of potential suitors in one fell swoop, and turn away when introduced to another Lee in a bar.

"You are considered an illustrious visitor. It's not every day that someone from Spain comes here," says Miss Sim, who's wearing traditional Korean clothing. "Yes, an illustrious guest of our Dear Leader," adds Mr. Park. The government has chosen to put me up in the Yanggakdo Hotel, a massive forty-two-story building with a thousand rooms—only a dozen of them occupied—in the middle of the Taedong River. The hotel reception area is papered with photographs and supposedly historical documents about the abuses committed by the Americans and Japanese on the Korean Peninsula. My two guides get out of the car and collect their luggage, and for a moment I have the sensation that we're all going on vacation together.

"To ensure your safety and well-being, we'll sleep in the rooms beside yours until you leave," says Mr. Park.

"Yes, for your safety," says Miss Sim.

Also for my safety, the back door of the hotel has been padlocked, and there's always someone watching the front door to make sure none of the guests leave without their spy guides. Darkness is a vast prison guarded by 1.2 million soldiers, 200,000 police officers, and thousands of informants. No one can leave or enter without its wardens' permission. The sirens go off promptly at dawn each morning, and a shrill voice penetrates the bedrooms through the loudspeakers mounted on every apartment building. "The revolution is a daily task!" "We must be faithful to the Great Leader." "We shall build a powerful socialist state!" It is the call of the Dear Leader, the beginning of a new day in the last pure Stalinist paradise on earth, an unparalleled theme park of tyranny that's got it all, from gulags and torture chambers to re-education camps for minds led astray and laboratories for weapons of mass destruction.

I think I'm going to enjoy myself here.

My first day in Kimland begins with paying obligatory homage to the sire of this political anomaly. We leave right on time; my guides show me where I should buy a bouquet of flowers and ask me to kneel before the statue of the Great Leader. The country has been in mourning more than three thousand days, but the people are still weeping for him on street corners, at the foot of his statue, on visits to the village where he was born, and in the state museums, where the guides are experts at telling emotional tales of the life of King Il-sung, incredible biographical fantasies, in endless accounts that go on and on until the listeners break out in tears.

Everyone, without exception, wears a pin with the image of one of the two Kims. Their portraits hang in schools, factories, and offices, in subway stations, in the streets, and in every home. And if one were to take the regime's word for it, far from being tired of the sight of their despots, the North Koreans value those portraits above their own lives. I still have a clipping of a bizarre dispatch from the Korean Central News Agency (KCNA) that describes how, after a train exploded as it passed through Ryongchon in April 2004 and hundreds of people died, the survivors tried to save the images of the Dear Leader from their homes "before searching for their family members or rescuing their possessions."

Kim the younger is omnipresent on local television, always with his perm (according to legend, he ordered the execution of a barber who didn't get his haircut right), his boots with lifts to make him taller, his olive green suit, and his large square glasses. Kim at the opening of a factory, Kim presiding over the meeting of some committee, Kim receiving the adoring applause of the people. Kim, Kim, Kim . . . At night, in my dreams, I wangle an interview with Kim

Jong-il. We're sitting in a large room hung with portraits of his father and we're talking about movies and women, his two great passions, as we drink one of the ten thousand grand reserve bottles from his personal cellar. I try to ask a question, but my mind goes blank. He looks at me and laughs.

"Did you want to ask something?" he's saying as I wake up from my dream.

We visit a library, where thousands of young people are studying the books written by the Kims. I buy two by Kim the younger: *On the Art of the Cinema* and his handbook on good journalism, in which he criticizes reporters for their inability to "adequately disseminate the revolutionary thoughts of the Great Leader." I should have bought a few more copies to give to colleagues who complain about the difficulties of the profession. For a North Korean reporter, jail awaits not for criticizing the regime—nobody's crazy enough to go that far—but for not praising it with sufficient revolutionary passion.

Finally, Mr. Park and Miss Sim show me a garden full of red begonias called *kimjongilias* in honor of Kim the younger, and another garden of purple orchids called *kimilsungias* in honor of Kim the elder. The only place not embellished with the image of the leader is the country's legal tender, because his face would be wrinkled, spoiled, handled as if he were just anybody.

"What do you think about your trip's itinerary so far?" asks Mr. Park long after I've overdosed on dictator-related visits.

"Honestly?" I ask in response.

"Yes, of course," he says. "Truth is very important to us Koreans. Truth is a clear pond and falsehood is a murky pond. You can only see through the clean water of truth."

"The itinerary is exhaustingly revolutionary," I say. "Frankly, I've had enough of revolutionary monuments and portraits of the Kims. Do you know that last night I dreamed about the Dear Leader?"

Mr. Park can tell I'm not happy with the sightseeing and asks what would make me happy. Going to a normal street, seeing people, I tell him. "All right, I'll speak with the Office and we'll see what we can do."

"Good night."

"Good night."

In the basement of the Yanggakdo Hotel, they've opened a small casino—run, of course, by Chinese businessmen. It has half a dozen Chinese women dressed in striking red outfits, two or three gaming tables, and a few slot machines. The casino is the beginning of what claims to be the opening of North Korea, along with the end of rationing, the liberalization of the prices of some goods, and plans to create a Special Economic Zone in which to experiment with the Chinese economic model. Leaders in Beijing, who are not eager to see a strong, democratic, and unified Korea on its borders, have advised their ally to apply the treatment that has worked so well for them: communism without equality, capitalism without freedom. But Kim Jong-il has his doubts: if I don't open the country up eventually, my kingdom will fall apart and I could end up like Ceausescu, arrested, humiliated, and executed by the people to whom I've caused so much suffering. After all, my country is a marvelous blend of Comrade Ceausescu's Romania, Maoist China, and Stalin's Soviet Union, all topped off with a few of my own special innovations. On the other hand, if I open the country, people will begin to learn about the outside world, find out that we're international pariahs, and discover my fondness for Mercedes, high-end Swiss watches, and good wine—I could end up like good old Ceausescu anyway. What to do?

While Kim Jong-il makes up his mind, the country keeps living up to the lag in its calendar. Calling this the year 92 doesn't seem so far off. Nothing is of this era. The people's clothing, the few Soviet cars that occasionally appear on the streets, the factories—all are straight out of a book on the Industrial Revolution. I've surreptitiously taken a few photos of the casino, and the guards have found me out. The photos aren't very good, but they're good enough for an article—"All in Red in North Korea"—and I'd like to keep them. The police officer summoned to deal with the matter searches in vain for the film, examines the camera, turns it over in his hands, presses various buttons, and gives up. "Film?" he asks. I shrug my shoulders and neglect to tell him it's a digital camera, since it's clear he's never encountered one and I see a chance of saving my work. He returns the camera and says, "It's Japanese, right?"

Another day in Darkness. Miss Sim and Mr. Park take me to Restaurant Street, where Pyongyang's handful of eateries are. We go into one, not necessarily the saddest of the lot. All of them, in fact, are empty. I've had certain reservations about North Korean cuisine ever since I visited Yanji, a town on the border between China and North Korea, where they served me a fish that was still very much alive. When my guide, Lin, and I had eaten half of it, the fish was still incomprehensibly thrashing its tail.

"We Koreans like fresh fish," said Lin, who'd managed to escape North Korea a few years earlier and made a living exporting Chinese products to his country.

In the restaurant they seat the three of us at a table for ten, and half a dozen waitresses start bringing plates of food until there's not an empty spot left on the table. The government doesn't want its visitors to leave thinking that food is scarce in North Korea, and my hosts insist on making every meal a Roman feast. The banquet is hard to stomach for anyone who's seen an orphanage in this country, with North Korean children dying for lack of a simple crust of bread. In the last five years of economic disaster, somewhere between one and two million people have died in a famine that has no witnesses. Somewhere between one and two million? It's an imprecise, dehumanized way to deal with individual lives, but in truth no one knows how many victims there are. We're not talking about the kind of famine we see in Africa, with television cameras and yearly concerts and pop stars who ask dying Africans, even Muslims in Sudan, whether they know it's Christmas. No, those who die in North Korea's famine are never seen. Only Kim Jong-il is omnipresent in the midst of this tragedy, with his enormous belly, round and satisfied, a symbol of repression ad absurdum. The only fat man in a country of starving people.

Second-to-last day in Kimland. The Office has planned a visit to the border between the two Koreas. The four-lane highway from Pyongyang to the Demilitarized Zone that separates the two enemies is smoothly paved and perfectly straight. It could be a European highway except for one tiny detail: it has no cars. In more than 170 kilometers, we haven't seen any other vehicles. Not one. Officially, there are only three ways a North Korean can acquire a private vehicle: winning a gold Olympic medal or similar international honor, holding a powerful position in government, or receiving the car as a personal gift from Kim Jong-il. North Koreans always walk: they walk everywhere, tens of kilometers if they have to. Children may spend hours walking to school and two hours in the classroom, and then start walking again to get home before nightfall.

After an eerie trip in which it sometimes seems like the world has ended, Mr. Park, Miss Sim, Park the driver, and the "honorary paper salesman" (me) arrive in our brand-new Mercedes in Panmunjom, the border town that for decades has symbolized like no other place the divide between the two Koreas. The North Korean and South Korean soldiers stationed here have been trained to forget that the soldiers posted on the other side are their brothers, speak the same language, and are part of the same nation. The Korean War (1950–1953) is not over, since no peace treaty was ever signed, only an armistice. "It was a stalemate," I suggest to break the ice.

"Are you saying we didn't win the war?" Miss Sim asks, offended.

"Well," I say, trying to downplay my comment, "there was a ceasefire and the borders remained basically the same as they'd been before the war."

"But we won the war," Miss Sim insists, her face anxious and her voice losing for the first time its accustomed sweetness. "We won it thanks to the Great Leader. How can you say we didn't win it when it's right in the books?"

"What books?" I ask, losing patience for a moment. "Outside of North Korea, there are other books, other worlds, other ways of seeing things. Miss Sim, don't believe everything you read."

I'm only arguing with Miss Sim about the war because I've decided that Mr. Park is a lost cause. He really believes the official propaganda, and my endless, needling discussions with him go nowhere. I like Miss Sim, though, and I suspect she knows that the war ended in a tie and that the country she lives in is intolerable. Her mother was a dancer, too, and during her career she traveled through a few Eastern European countries, Russia, and Mongolia.

She always came back home with the latest pop music, which she'd bought in secret. Since her retirement a decade ago, though, she hasn't been able to buy more cassettes for her daughter. For Miss Sim, her mother's trips had been her only contact with the outside world, and, although that contact was very limited, it was much greater than that of her fellow countrymen, maybe great enough to have made her understand the absurdity of the place it is her fate to inhabit. We end our political discussion and I ask her what music she likes. She tells me that the last thing her mother brought back was a compilation of Michael Jackson songs. I tease her and tell her she's a bit out of date.

"Will you bring me some music when you come back?" she asks me.

"If they let me come back, yes, I'll bring you a CD of music."

"Not a CD," she says. "A tape. I don't have . . ."

"All right, then, a tape."

The end of the Second World War meant an end to Japan's dreams of empire and the withdrawal of Japanese troops from Korea. The Russians took advantage of the vacuum to occupy the north, while the Americans hastily sought to shore up their influence in the south. The two victors decided to split the territory between them and selected the thirty-eighth parallel as the dividing line. In 1950 the North tried to force reunification by invading the South. The first part of the war was a cakewalk for communist Korea, which nearly seized control of the entire peninsula. The second part, which began with the historic landing of McArthur's troops in Inchon, was a cakewalk for the South, which also almost gained total control. McArthur dreamed of that victory and even dreamed of continuing to the gates of China itself, where Mao had decided to sacrifice thousands of his soldiers to save North Korea. In the end, all the death and sacrifice of both parties only brought them back to where they'd started: the thirty-eighth parallel. "A stalemate," I'd say. "An irrefutable victory for the North," according to Miss Sim. A defeat for both, most likely. As a result, millions of families remain divided today on either side. The North, hostage to those determined to impose one way of thinking on its citizens, stopped the clock of progress and took the path of repression. The South, having survived the military dictatorship, headed toward the future and focused its efforts on creating a modern democratic nation, flawed like any other, of course, but one where no one ends up in a gulag for expressing an opinion. Over time, and with such different approaches to development, the thirty-eighth parallel no longer separates one country into two opposing systems but instead marks the boundary between two worlds.

Darkness.

Light.

If one could make the trip, walk from one side to the other, it would be an incredible journey. A North Korean could walk fifty meters and advance a century. A South Korean could walk the same distance and go back in time: to year 92. But it's not easy to escape the grip of the most tyrannical dictator of our times, elude the soldiers of the most repressive army on earth, and leave the world's most hermetic country. The regime's prisons are full of North Koreans who have attempted that journey, tried to leave the Kims' paradise and make it to the Light. Fleeing south isn't an option, because the border is impassable. The Yellow Sea is to the west and the Sea of Japan to the east, neither navigable without a halfway decent boat. The only possible exit, then, is to the north: to enter China and seek a way into South Korea from there.

The Tumen River traces the border between China and North Korea along much of the Chinese province of Jilin. If you watch the border at a fordable point, it won't be long before you spot a group of North Koreans trying to cross. Here, too, life turns on the seasons. Frost. Thaw. Falling temperatures freeze the water and turn the river into a silvery carpet that can be crossed to freedom, as long as the sheet of ice beneath your feet is thick enough. When warm temperatures return and the waters get moving again, defectors swim the river to China. Crossing the Tumen River is itself a paradox: fleeing one dictatorship to enter another. If you manage to throw off the North Korean soldiers, there's still the chance that the Chinese will find you. Beijing, in an attempt to placate its ally and friend, sends captured North Korean refugees back to their country, well aware that they'll be condemned to forced labor camps. The hands of the residents of Chinese border towns are tied, as the Chinese government has made it a crime to aid or shelter any North Korean refugee. No humanitarian organization is authorized to help the thousands of people who arrive. But it's far worse to endure hunger, to watch your loved ones die and be unable to do anything about it. There comes a time when the risk of trying to escape pales in comparison to the risk of staying.

Kim weighed both options and decided to leave. I met him next to the Tumen River, on the Chinese side, soon after he'd fled from Darkness.

The first thing I notice about Kim is his size: he's thirteen years old, but he doesn't look older than ten. I'm also surprised to find him alone, because North Koreans usually organize their escapes in small groups so they can help each other. It's no journey for a lone adventurer, much less one who's a kid. Kim has never seen the ocean and doesn't know how to swim, and when he reaches the banks of the Tumen River after a long twenty-five-kilometer walk, he must somehow cross to the other side. It's September, and the water has not yet frozen. He hides behind some bushes for four days, unsure whether to cross or not, afraid that he'll be discovered. If he doesn't cross soon, he could starve to death right there; if he crosses, he might drown. At the point he's chosen, the distance between the two banks is barely fifty meters. On the fifth night, afraid his time and options will run out while he's hesitating, he grabs a plank of wood and starts kicking his feet until he reaches the opposite shore, exhausted, hungry, and soaking wet. He's escaped North Korea.

The Fangs, a family that lives near the border post in the city of Tumen, find Kim near their house. As soon as she sees him huddled next to the sign announcing that he's arrived in China, Mrs. Fang pours a bucket of water on him to wake him and hurries him away before the guards spot him. A few meters away is the Chinese police's refugee detention center, which processes the handover of captured North Koreans to the soldiers on the other side. Mrs. Fang takes little Kim to her house, hides him, heals the bruises all over his body, and feeds him four times a day. Little by little, his body begins to resemble those of the living. The Kim I've met is not the same one who managed to leave the Dear Leader three weeks earlier.

"When he arrived, you could see his bones," Mrs. Fang tells me proudly, pinching Kim's cheek. "Now look at him, he's small but there's meat on those bones. Sometimes he even smiles."

The Fangs run a small grocery store near the border. They have a son a little older than Kim, and the family moved in with Mr. Fang's parents two years ago. Mr. Fang objected at first to the arrival of one more mouth to feed, afraid that his wife's new charity project would get them in trouble with the authorities. At last, he reluctantly agreed to let Kim stay until he's strong enough to start the journey back to North Korea.

The boy hardly said a word during his first week in China; all he did was eat and sleep. He didn't let anyone touch him, change his clothes, or bathe him. The Fangs didn't know where he was from, how long he'd been traveling, or where his family was. It was a week before Kim started telling his story, and when he finally did, Mrs. Fang constantly interrupted him with exclamations of "That's why we have to help these people" and "The world is such a cruel place." She looked smugly at her husband, satisfied that her generosity had been justified once more.

"Well, what are we supposed to do?" she asks when her husband complains about her effort to help the North Korean refugees. "Let them die, these poor people who don't have anywhere to go?"

Kim tells the Fangs that he was born in a small city of five thousand a two-day walk from the border. The town had endured two years of scarcity and rationing, but in the winter of 1998 the situation had become intolerable. The government rations became more and more limited and, without warning, stopped arriving at all that December. There was nothing to eat and nothing to grow. Kim confirms for the first time something I've only read before, one of those things I had to hear several times, from a number of people, before I could believe them.

"In my town we ate tree bark and grass," he tells me. "But people got sick to their stomachs and babies couldn't digest the food. There wasn't anything else, so we softened the bark with water so it would be easier to swallow. Lots of people died of diarrhea and other illnesses."

The famine stretched on another three years. The residents of Kim's town started dying of hunger, one by one, and no aid came. Before the previous winter had ended, half the population had died and the other half was on its way. Without heat or electricity, the townspeople wondered, which will kill our children first, cold or hunger?

Kim describes scenes of dying people wandering like zombies until they fell to the ground. Local officials left, assuring people that they were going to Pyongyang to ask for help. Nobody saw them again. The adults, determined to give their children what little they had, were the first to die. But this made things worse, since the children were left orphaned and had to take care of themselves. Mothers who had recently given birth nursed as many babies as they could, whether their own or not. The town, abandoned to its fate, was dying. All activity ceased. Everyone's energy was focused on finding food, but the last winter had been so harsh, with temperatures as low as twenty degrees below zero, that even the insects and the rats seemed to have disappeared. Ice had halted the rivers, frost covered the fields, and life had vanished as far as the eye could see.

Kim's father died in the famine, leaving his mother to take care of the four children.

"My mother gave everything she had to eat to me and my siblings. She told me I had to survive so I could take care of the others. One day she got sick and slowly grew weaker until she also died."

The townspeople who survived the winter met up during the summer and organized three or four groups of young people, some of them children, who were still standing. They were to cross the border into China, look for food, and return as soon as possible. Kim volunteered and joined a group of four other boys, all around his age. He'd made the trip with his group, but he was the only one to reach the other side. One night, as they drew near the border, they heard the voices of the soldiers and all ran to hide. At dawn, only he was left.

"I think the others were captured," Kim says.

Many Chinese families in the towns near the border try to help the refugees despite the official prohibition, giving them food and sometimes offering temporary shelter to the people who come to their doors. Mrs. Fang has become one of the most active. China, after all, suffered one of the greatest famines in history only a few decades ago. The elderly still remember how they suffered during that period, and the young have heard dozens of stories about those days of privation. It's because of the famine that the Chinese now have a well-deserved reputation for eating anything on four legs that isn't a table and anything that flies that isn't a plane. Hunger expanded the Chinese menu to include dog, rat, and insects, which have become delicacies in some parts of the country.

It was unimaginable, but decades after Mao Zedong's Great Leap Forward, yet another unbalanced leader full of revolutionary fantasies was bringing his nation to its knees with another massive famine, stubbornly determined to prove man's inability to learn from the past. What made Kim Jong-il all the crueler was that Mao, at least, had believed his fantasies. The Dear Leader and his coterie of military men and government officials living the good life in Pyongyang do not. Theirs is a regime based on a massive deception. The struggle against those born into privilege has been halted to create the first hereditary communist dynasty in history. The equitable distribution of wealth has given way to the unrestrained extravagance of leaders who live like emperors while feeding their people only Marxist ideology. The principles of communism are upheld by a Mafioso state funded by international smuggling of arms, drugs, cars, and anything else, legal or not, that can be sold. The North Korean elite, which may at one point have been motivated by ideas, has gradually degenerated and is now irresistibly drawn to capitalist materialism. You can see them landing at the Pyongyang airport, recently arrived from Beijing, toting color televisions, bottles of cognac, and Hollywood movies, everything forbidden to the rest of their people.

Mrs. Fang is only in her forties, too young to have experienced the famine of the Great Leap Forward, but she feels an irrepressible need to help the refugees. She's learned a smattering of Korean through her contact with the new arrivals, whom she always offers something to eat, hot tea, or some instant noodles. Among the people she takes in are doctors and police officers, engineers and soldiers, schoolteachers and disenchanted government officials. Above all, there are women, and Mrs. Fang tries to let them know: you are the only ones who will be welcomed with open arms.

The shortage of women in China, caused by decades of the infanticide and abortion of millions of females, has created a generation of bachelors who are having more and more difficulty finding partners. The North Korean women who make it across the Tumen River have become an easy solution. Lin, the guide who on a previous trip to the border had taken me to discover how fresh the North Koreans like their fish, also showed me how the trade in women works. He had good contacts with the trafficking networks set up on both sides of the border. One day, if he could save up enough money, he too planned to buy a wife. He took me to an abandoned building on the outskirts of Yanji, an hour by car from the border, where we met two intermediaries who were acquaintances of his. The apartment was divided into small compartments where more than twenty women were waiting for potential buyers to arrive. The two men who ran the business complained that times were tough. Police raids had become more frequent, and thousands of women were being sent back to North Korea. While in the past the businessmen had been able to weasel out of human trafficking charges by paying a small fine, the crime could now get them sent to jail or even cost them their lives.

"Come on in, take a look at what we've got," one of them said, pulling back curtains to reveal the place where several young women were waiting.

The walls of the apartment had been decorated with photographs of beautiful Korean actresses. A radiator and some blankets served to protect the women from the cold. They were fed three times a day so they'd gain weight and given some makeup and clothing that wasn't too provocative, so as not to offend anyone who came looking for a meek housewife. They were all waiting nervously for someone to come and take them away. Soo Yun had crossed the border a year before. She arrived in China famished and weak, and no sooner had she set foot in the country than she was contacted by a group of men offering to help. For three weeks they fed her, gave her clean clothing, and took care of her. She thought her luck had turned at last. One day they took her to an abandoned factory in Yanji and put her on the wife market. A man offered three thousand yuan, a little less than five hundred dollars at the time, for her, and two days later they were married in his hometown in a ceremony with dozens of guests in attendance and a large reception.

"I couldn't refuse, or they'd have sent me back to North Korea," Soo Yun told me when I met her, still living with her husband and about to give birth to their first child.

She was twenty-three years old. Thanks to her new life in China, she was able to keep the family she'd left behind in North Korea alive.

"My husband isn't a bad man," she said. "He treats me well, and, anyway, what choice do I have?"

Soo Yun could consider herself lucky. Most of the wife-buyers in Jilin were old men, had some physical or mental deficiencies, or had come from the countryside, without economic resources or education, to spend their life savings on a wife. Afraid that the police would discover that their wives were refugees and force them to return their purchase, it wasn't unusual for them to keep the women inside day and night, out of everyone's sight. Soo Yun, on the other hand, had been accepted by her husband's community because the dearth of women was threatening the town with extinction. The police would have had to arrest every single one of its inhabitants to take her away.

North Korean women who are deported and sent back to Kimland are considered traitors. Article 47 of the North Korean penal code declares anyone who flees the country an "enemy of the state," and their children born in relationships with men in the other country are seen as part of the future enemy, introduced into the country to undermine the purity of North Korean society. In recent years, the organization Human Rights Without Frontiers has gathered testimony from women who had been sent back and after a number of years in prison managed to escape to South Korea and tell their story: prisoners forced to kill their cellmates' children to avoid being tortured, newborns placed in plastic bags that were sealed off with their mothers' umbilical cords, other babies hung head down in the prison yard until they died. Once again I found it hard to believe that such evil could exist, even in a sick mind. Only the repetition of similar testimonies from women who didn't know each other finally convinced me. It was happening again, and like so many times before, in Nazi Germany, Cambodia, or Rwanda, the rest of the world seemed incapable of taking notice before it was too late.

Kim has recovered quickly under Mrs. Fang's ministrations. His skin is pink with life again, his eyes shine, and his legs are strong enough to support him without assistance. It's time for him to go back to be with his siblings, who are waiting for him in the village in North Korea. Kim is happy to be in China—he never imagined it was possible to eat so much—but he feels restless. He wants to leave as soon as possible to bring food to his town. He's afraid that if he delays any longer, there won't be anyone left alive. The Fangs have asked him to stay a few days more until he's gotten all his strength back. Even Mr. Fang enjoys the boy's company and accepts his presence, despite the risk that the police could come looking for trouble. But Kim is insistent, so Mrs. Fang prepares everything for his trip. She's bought two backpacks and filled them with things that could help their North Korean neighbors. They've got to be things that don't weigh too much but can keep people alive as long as possible. Instant noodles, sugar, dried fruit, flour, powdered milk. One question remains: how will he make it back to North Korea?

It's not easy to enter the world's most hermetic country, elude the soldiers of the most repressive army on earth, return to the most tyrannical dictator of our times. The trip back presents even more challenges than the journey out. Temperatures have fallen, not enough to freeze the river but enough to chill its waters and make the crossing more difficult. They consider improvising a small raft of some sort but discard the idea: the current could take it downriver, and the soldiers would spot it easily. Mrs. Fang has heard of places where the water level falls dramatically at this time of year and hardly comes up to one's knees.

"You can just walk across the river," she says. "But that's also where soldiers are keeping a closer eye on things."

Kim's greatest worry is that the border guards will discover him and keep all the food for themselves. The NGOs accuse Kim Jong-il of distributing foreign humanitarian aid to his troops to keep them loyal; even though they get enough to eat, food is still of particular interest to them, as it can be sold for good money on the black market. The soldiers wouldn't hesitate to keep it and send Kim to a forced labor camp. Going back home with nothing, weeks after he'd left, would mean failure and humiliation.

On the day he is to leave, they all agree that Kim will only walk at night and hide during the day. If he sees soldiers, he is to return to the Fangs' home. Once he's in North Korea, he should get away from the border as quickly as he can. Several other women add to Mrs. Fang's gifts with extra supplies for the journey. We accompany him to the riverbank, and the neighbors show him the road he should take to find the low area of the river. Kim hoists his bags to his back and starts to walk. Slowly he disappears into the distance, going deeper into Darkness until he vanishes altogether. I've never found out whether he made it home or whether, if he did, there was anyone left to save in his dying town. Three years would pass before it would be my turn to enter North Korea, on a trip that would help me understand like never before what had driven little Kim, and so many other North Koreans like him, to flee their own country.

Mr. Park and Miss Sim want my last day in North Korea to be unforgettable. They've got good news. My request for a visit to "a normal street" has been approved, so we drive to a nondescript avenue and get out of the car. They ask me not to take photos.

"They told us there was an incident in the casino," says Mr. Park, reprimanding me gently, "and we'd appreciate it if it didn't happen again. You're allowed to take pictures of the buildings, but not of the people. We North Koreans don't like to have our photo taken."

We walk down a sad street full of people dressed in sad clothing, with a few sad businesses on either side of the street. There's nothing to sell, nothing to buy. A butcher has a refrigerated case with a single piece of calf's meat waiting for some lucky soul. People walk back and forth, no laughter or smiles, only monotony. A few children, startled by their first sight of a Westerner with a big nose and white skin, run in fright or hurl themselves into their mothers' arms. An old man spits what are clearly revolutionary insults when he sees me pass, which Miss Sim genially translates as greetings from the "friendly people of North Korea." If I come back, I think, I'll have to remember to bring some modern music for Miss Sim. She's been very good to me on this trip. I muse that if she's really aware of the place she lives in, life must be especially hard for her.

At night they've prepared me a special feast, larger than the previous ones and even harder to stomach. For the third time, Miss Sim puts on her traditional Korean garb; Mr. Park puts on a tie. The driver, Mr. Park, joins us. The desserts arrive, and Mr. Park, the guide, takes advantage of his companions' momentary distraction to ask me a question he must have been carrying inside him for years but hasn't ever had the chance to ask. He's waited for the last night of the last day to ask it now.

"How do they really live in the South?"

The question leaves me somewhat disconcerted. We both know that over the last few days we've been actors, each of us playing his part, and I get the feeling that Mr. Park is asking—just for a moment—for us to take off our masks and be honest. Is it possible that he knows, too?

"The people on the other side," I tell him, "are free to enter and leave their country as they please. There are poor people, yes, but nobody goes hungry and the heating works in wintertime. Nobody is afraid of the government: the government is afraid of the people. Politicians can be fired if citizens don't like the way they do their job. South Korea is admired around the world. Its televisions, cars, and merchant ships are sold in America and Europe. It's a modern country and, above all, it's a free country . . ."

Mr. Park is silent. He doesn't ask any more questions, our brief venture into honesty at an end.

The next day they accompany me to the airport. Mr. Park says, "I hope you didn't get the wrong impression of our country." Miss Sim says, "Yes, we hope you have a good impression of our country."

They both say, "Come back soon." I wait for my plane to take off from the runway of the Pyongyang-Sunan airport, and when I look out the window I find myself face to face once more with the image of the Great Leader that graces the façade of the terminal. I sigh with relief that I'm going to lose sight of them both, him and his son. It's so easy for me. To come, to see, to leave again. It's so different for those who stay. In a world divided between light and shadows, where dreams depend on the seasons and the road to freedom can be a frozen river, the North Koreans live trapped in the darkest corner of the human condition, where despair and tyranny dwell together.

Chaojun

Yang Weiqi and Zhu Li's only chance was born a girl. There would be no more children for them, as China's birth policy only allowed them one. The doctors at Changhai Hospital in Shanghai handed the infant to her parents with a look on their faces as if they were about to announce that a patient had gone on to a better life. "Don't fret, maybe in the future the government will let you have another and it will be a boy." For Yang Weiqi, though, one look at his daughter was enough to make him discard the centuries-long traditional preference for males in Chinese culture. He wouldn't exchange his little girl for anything or anybody in the world.

"She'll be better than a man," he said.

And so the little girl was named: Chaojun, which means "Better than a man."

The couple had met in Qingdao, in Shangdong Province. He was working as an industrial mechanic, a job that cost him his right index finger, severed in an accident, and she was an accountant in an electronics factory. In 1993, they married and went to live the dream of a new China in Shanghai. Hoping to climb the social ladder and enter the burgeoning Chinese middle class, they had from the beginning pinned their hopes on that skinny, nervous little girl with lively eyes. They wanted to give her the opportunities they'd never had in life, working only for her and investing every last yuan of their savings in her education. Mr. Yang gave Chaojun attention he'd never have given a son, determined to fulfill the promise he'd made with his daughter's name—that she'd be better than a man—and knowing that she would have to work twice as hard if she wanted to make it. Make it to where? He had no idea. Success, or what it might mean, was a remote, inaccessible place for him, but he knew he wanted his daughter to reach it. He decided that music would take her there.

Classical music had been yet another victim of Mao Zedong's purges during the Cultural Revolution of the '60s and '70s. Like other cultural artifacts, it was prohibited, and anyone who played it was persecuted by the Red Guards. Conservatories were closed and instruments burned. People who knew how to play an instrument had to hide their ability to avoid public humiliation and punishment. With the death of the Great Helmsman and the economic opening that followed, however, music was brought back to Chinese life, and in short order it became the preferred activity for millions of parents seeking excellence in their only children, their only chances.

These days, thousands of families travel to Beijing and Shanghai, ready to bet it all on admission to the conservatory. On entrance examination days, you can see the parents lining up to try to get one of the limited number of spots available each year, offering all their savings as a bribe to buy a way in and weeping when their child is rejected. Becoming a pianist isn't the automatic leap to fame enjoyed by athletes who win Olympic medals, but it guarantees a comfortable future and respect for the family. It doesn't matter whether the parents' only son has to play until his fingers ache and he can hardly sit up. Dreams have always required extra effort in China, if only because of the stubborn law of probabilities, which makes it so difficult to stand out among hundreds of millions of compatriots. Parents see the piano as a springboard to status in this country, which has fully recovered its class consciousness (if it ever lost it in the first place). Children's aspirations are nothing more than a reflection of their parents' dreams, which were all too often cut short in the past, in a China that punished individual ambitions and interpreted the quest for excellence as evidence of selfishness and individualism.

Mr. Yang tried first with the violin. He gave one to his daughter for her fourth birthday. Chaojun practiced for months until she finally had to quit because the posture for playing caused terrible neck pain. Her father didn't give up. He took all his savings, almost one thousand dollars, borrowed money from family and friends, and bought a battered, used piano, hopelessly out of tune. With the money left over, he hired Professor Lin, one of the best teachers at the Shanghai Conservatory of Music, and spent his last yuan on lessons. Professor Lin assured her parents that the little girl had talent. "Nice work, Chaojun," he'd say on days when he refused his fee, aware that the family couldn't afford to pay almost forty dollars an hour for classes. Afterward, in her free time, Chaojun would practice and practice the exercises until she was exhausted. At bedtime, instead of stories, sheet music.

When the Yangs look back on the last four years of poverty, they are convinced that all their sacrifices have been worth it. Chaojun, just nine years old, is a little star now. When I hear her play for the first time in the spring of 2004, she's a student at the Children's Palace, a colonial mansion on Yan'an Road in Shanghai that Soong Ching Ling, widow of nationalist leader Sun Yat Sen, turned into a school in 1953. The center, also known as the Little Emperors Palace, was originally intended to educate poor children but over time has become the place where the new Chinese elite send their children to learn music, Chinese calligraphy, painting, or drama. The one-child policy of recent decades has prevented the births of 400 million Chinese, leading to the abortion or infanticide of tens of millions of girls and transforming the concept of family in China. In Shanghai and other wealthier cities on the east coast, the law has created a generation of pampered only children, little emperors for whom nothing is enough and whose parents demand that their children, in return for being spoiled, try their hardest to fulfill the aspirations they've inherited.

Tiny ballerinas are getting ready for their lesson at the Little Emperors Palace, stretching like vain swans, raising their arms as they turn, their feet nimble on the parquet floor. The afternoon light streams in through the mansion's large windows as the mothers chase their daughters around the room, smoothing their ponytails and adjusting their outfits one last time. Obese children, a rarity in China only a few years ago, are playing the trombone in the room next door. In the background I hear a vocal class, where fifty children are singing arias for a group of American tourists. A piano sounds faintly in the distance. Following its notes to a corner of the third floor, I find Chaojun sitting at the piano. Her fingers glide across the keyboard, each moving independently of the others, stopping on this or that key with the precision of an assembly line robot. Her eyes are closed, the sheet music forgotten: Chaojun has played Bach's second prelude many times.

"It's my favorite," she says, her fingers still moving over the piano.

Her father, Yang Weiqi, is beside her, listening as if for the first time. He has the face of a Chinese peasant, leathery from years of work outdoors, his brown skin tanned by the sun, and a friendly, rural manner that persists despite his years in the city. Although the Little Emperors Palace has become an elite place, the school still accepts children from poorer families who have special abilities, allowing them to attend classes at half-price. Chaojun is performing this afternoon, and she's come here to practice. A number of government officials will be there, so it's an important day for the family. Chaojun made it to level ten at the Shanghai Conservatory of Music at only eight years old, making her the youngest professional musician in the country. In 2001 she won her first national competition and since then has given concerts in Austria, Australia, South Korea, Hong Kong, and Paris, which she visited with an official delegation headed by the mayor of Shanghai in its bid to host the World's Fair in 2010. "I played the piano for three hundred people from eighty-eight countries. It was the biggest day of my career," says Chaojun, remembering the pomp surrounding her recital in France. Brief television pieces and newspaper articles about the "child prodigy from Shanghai" have given her a certain amount of celebrity in the city's cultural circles, and she seems to accept the attention as an inevitable part of her destiny. High-ranking officials from the local Communist Party count on her for government celebrations, displaying her as an example of the educational system and a symbol of the new China. The doors of the Shanghai theaters have opened to

Chaojun when other girls her age are still playing with dolls.

All of this is seen as a success—partly because of how improbable it is—for a family that arrived in Shanghai from the countryside eleven years ago, empty-handed. The city of opportunities has lived up to the legend, at least for them, and Mr. Yang is thankful every day that he had the courage to choose a new life in one of the few places where a daughter could be "better than a man."

If all goes well, Chaojun will complete a journey begun a long time ago, and bring the efforts of three generations of women to fulfillment. Her grandmother, Pan Sulian, was the first. She gave her children a good start in life despite her origins in a destitute village in Qingdao that had no electricity or running water. It was there she met the soldier from the People's Liberation Army who would become her husband. China was a broken, divided empire at the time, sunk in poverty and ignorance, a shadow of the thousand-year-old culture that centuries before had been the most advanced civilization on earth. When Mao triumphantly entered Beijing in 1949, bringing the chaos and civil war to an end, Pan Sulian and the rest of the Chinese celebrated it as a new dawn. The Great Helmsman had brought pride to China once more. He would unite the country and heal the open wounds of a century of humiliation that had begun in the mid-nineteenth century with the British intervention, continued festering with the Japanese occupation, and closed at last with the communist victory. Mao helped the Chinese walk with their heads held high again, but in exchange he robbed them of their freedom, manipulated their lives, ruined the country, and sank his people into a world of shadows. The famines and purges plunged China into a sort of national schizophrenia.

Chaojun's grandmother survived the worst years by working in a state-owned textile factory for ten dollars a month; her family avoided being sent off to the communes because her husband was a soldier. Zhu Li took up the baton next: she finished high school and found a job in an electronics plant in Qingdao in the first years of economic opening. Soon that factory and others would flood the world with their "Made in China" products. In those days, the world still didn't quite believe that China was waking up, and the majority of the Chinese were unaware how much their lives were going to change in the years to come. Communism had offered equality in exchange for freedom; Western capitalism had delivered freedom in exchange for equality. China, having initiated economic reforms in 1978, was going to try something new: communism without equality, capitalism without freedom. From the beginning it was clear that the political repression would continue and that the new economic liberalism was not going to offer the same opportunities to everyone. The country would be split between those who had climbed aboard the train of progress and those who had missed it. The result, however, was a place that was infinitely better, more socially free, and inarguably more prosperous than Mao's China.

Zhu Li worked twelve hours a day, seven days a week, for the next six years, sending part of her earnings to her parents back home, until she met the industrial mechanic who would become her husband, fell in love with him, and followed him in his adventure in Shanghai. "I was the first woman in the family to leave Qingdao," Zhu Li recalls. "When I got to the city, I couldn't believe what I was seeing, it was amazing. All those people in the streets, the tall buildings, the cars."

Now it is Chaojun's turn. The shared journey of three generations of women who have lived in three very different Chinas is coming to an end, and she is tasked with reaching the last stop. Of those Chinas, only Chaojun's would allow someone without wealth or connections to make something of herself in life. The little girl will have to make the last effort, run the final straightaway, and arrive at the finish line.

"My mother and I never imagined having the opportunities that Chaojun has," says Zhu Li as she serves tea in her home in Shanghai, a modest house beside the new shopping centers on Nanjing Road. "Back then, we were just trying to survive. We couldn't think about bigger things. Not being hungry, having clothes and a job—those were our greatest aspirations. We found happiness in the littlest things. Chaojun has the whole world in front of her."

Beside her mother, the little girl nods. She is playing Chopin's

Ballade No. 3. Her body sways from side to side, rocking to the rhythm of the notes, and she closes her eyes to keep time.

"She's always been high-strung," says her mother. "The piano is the only place where she can be calm."

"One day I'll be like Lang Lang," interrupts Chaojun, referring to the young Chinese pianist who ever since his debut at Carnegie Hall in 2001 has been acclaimed at concerts all over the world. "I'm going to be a pianist!"

"Play another piece for our guest," says Mr. Yang, while Zhu Li serves more tea and sweets.

"Hmm, would you like a little more Chopin?" Chaojun asks, shaking her braids off her shoulders, her fingers fluttering over the keyboard again.

My lack of musical knowledge prevents me from knowing whether the little pianist will be like Lang Lang or whether she'll be left by the wayside, but when she finishes the piece I ask her what she feels when she plays. I am surprised by her answer.

"Oh," she says. "I don't feel anything. I just play."

It would be difficult to find a more determined people than the Chinese, or one that has endured more to attain a better life. No one has given them anything. The Chinese feel that it's their turn to live in a land of opportunities, a place that, unlike Cambodia or the Philippines, has managed to shatter the leaden grip of poverty and move unflinchingly into the future. Once upon a time there weren't enough human traffickers to handle the thousands of Chinese citizens leaving for Europe, Australia, or the United States in search of a better life in the largest diaspora man has ever seen. Now, though, these traffickers are steadily being left without work. Opportunity is here, in China. Why leave? This is probably the most rapidly developing country in human history, raising millions of people out of poverty in the first thirty years of economic openness—though millions of peasants are still trapped in it—and making the Chinese awakening a reality at last, after so many failed attempts.

Famine and war are things of the past. The days when China hung its head before the world seem long gone now, and international leaders are lining up again for audiences with the new emperors. Long gone, too, are the humiliations of colonialism: today it is China that invades and subjugates regions like Tibet. Long gone are the days when its leaders believed that power came from the barrel of a gun: It's the economy, stupid! This has allowed China to occupy what it sees as its merited place in the world. And yet in the minds of those who run this country, an unshakeable belief remains, as if no time has passed: personal sacrifice should serve the collective good.

That idea has guided Asian societies, some more than others, over the course of their histories. It is one of the "Asian values" exploited by so many of the region's dictators to justify their continued grip on power and the oppression of their people. If society is more important than the individual, what's wrong with arresting those who go off script and try to row against the current? Isn't crushing the individual to achieve a harmonious society justified? Dictatorship was considered the natural state of things in Asia for centuries. In some parts of the West, the belief persists that democracy isn't possible in places like China because its citizens don't want it and, even if they do, they are not ready for it, as if values, a desire for freedom, and the ability to express one's thoughts or to choose the people to lead one's community were linked to the color of one's skin or one's place of birth.

Perhaps it is my own fascination with the idea of personal sacrifice for the good of the group that has brought me to the Yangtze over and over again. It's a strange sensation: visiting places that will soon cease to exist altogether. A red line painted by government officials passes through towns and cities at the river's edge, marking the houses, temples, schools, restaurants, streets, and memories that will be flooded when the Three Gorges Dam is finished. *Submersion line: 157.8 meters* says a sign in the city of Fengdu. A number of families wait on the small wharf by the riverbank for the boats that will take them far from here, to a new life. The government has told them they will be "relocated," like furniture that's in the way. The lucky ones will get a house built on the other side of the river, higher up, in the new Fengdu. The rest will be sent off to places designated by the authorities. They don't complain about not wanting to live in Inner Mongolia.

Since when has choosing been an option in a dictatorship?

Some of the townspeople have spent the last few days exhuming their dead and hauling off the remains. Ancestors are important in China: they're part of you, and you have to take care of them and look out for them in the other life. You can't just leave your great-great-grandfather behind. From the wharf, it's only a few meters' walk to the old part of the city—but that short trip takes you centuries back in time, to another China. Fengdu has been here, imperturbable, for 2,300 years. And now it's going to disappear, great-great-grandfathers and all.

A dozen people are sitting in a nameless little restaurant eating fried noodles, pork, and rice. They invite me in and make space at their table. Chinese food is not made for the solo traveler. The dishes are always large, the tables round—everything designed for sharing. We talk about the Three Gorges Dam, and they tell me it's a wonderful idea and that the government can't be wrong, it does everything for our benefit. They're not going to share any opinions to the contrary with a foreigner, and—worst of all—a journalist.

Since when has speaking freely been an option in a dictatorship?

Mrs. Jiang, a tiny, plump woman with large, rosy cheeks, runs the place.

"We have to close the business," she says matter-of-factly. "Sometimes life is like that."

Mrs. Jiang introduces me to her daughter and asks if I'd be interested in taking her to Europe with me—she's unmarried and a good cook, and I shouldn't worry about the wedding preparations, it can all be whipped up in a flash, tomorrow, even, if you're in a hurry. She gestures to an old portrait of Mao hanging on the wall. It's a clumsy rendering of the Great Helmsman, with a red heart beside him, painted on a sheet of glass and hung in a wooden frame.

"Mao, Mao, Mao," everyone in the restaurant starts chanting when they see me looking at it.

Mrs. Jiang climbs onto a chair, takes down the portrait, and offers it to me. She knows that the restaurant's days, that the days of life as she knows it, are numbered, and she's decided to save her daughter and Mao. I tell her I can only take the portrait, and she laughs.

"You're taking our Sun," she says, forgiving my snub.

I've never known what to do with the portrait of Mao. I'm fond of the gift, but I couldn't take seeing the image of the dictator, with its silly, rapturous smile, hanging on my office wall day and night. I've always criticized the people who buy key rings, figurines, and posters of Mao in the markets of Hong Kong or Beijing. It's what I call teddy-bear dictator syndrome, which makes us think of some tyrants with something like affection, like a mean-tempered but lovable grandfather. I've kept the portrait in a cabinet, among other souvenirs from my travels: the old Russian camera and tripod I bought in Jalalabad, the mask with the phallus-shaped nose that the Bhutanese hang above the doors of their houses to frighten off evil spirits, and the copy of Kim Jong-il's *On the Art of the Cinema* that I bought in Pyongyang.

The Three Gorges Dam is, in the eyes of Mao's successors, the second Great Wall. No matter that over the years suspicions have grown that the harm the dam will cause far outweighs its benefits. The Party says it's a vital project for the nation, proof of the greatness of the Chinese people. More than 20,000 peons work like ants on the 185-meter-tall wall. "Work harder, for the nation," urge the enormous signs on the slopes of the mountains around the colossal project. "Take pride in the Three Gorges Dam," says another. Chinese leaders have always dreamed of harnessing the Yangtze River. In the early 1920s, the nationalist leader Sun Yat Sen dreamed of building a great retaining wall, and in 1956 Mao wrote a poem that declared that "walls of stone will stand upstream to the west" of the river. Every few years, the monsoon winds bring great summer storms, the river floods, and thousands of people die. So the river must be curbed, dominated. Nothing is bigger than China, nothing is more powerful than the Party—not even you, Yangtze, who have given this nation so much and taken so much away.

In 1992, when Beijing's dictators decide to build the dam, they hit 1.5 million snags: the people who, ever since their ancestors first settled the area eight thousand years ago, have been building their lives on the river's banks. The official study on the project's impact suggests that the manmade lake created by the dam will stretch more than 600 kilometers and swallow 13 cities, 140 towns, and 1,352 small villages. History has lost count of the number of times that Chinese leaders have asked their people to sacrifice themselves for the common good, so one more effort isn't too much to ask. The leaders have rarely joined in that sacrifice, living their people's tragedies from a distance—but that's an insignificant detail, proof only that the Sky God has never intended for all his children to be equal. They start shuffling the 1.5 million snags from one side of the country to the other. It's the same story in every village. The police come, paint a line to mark where the water will reach, and ask the people to resign themselves to their fate, for the sake of the motherland. Everybody wants to salvage something. Mrs. Jiang wants to save Mao and her daughter. The Xias want to save memories of a life that's about to be submerged under the Yangtze River.

The Xias live in Yunyang County in the Chinese province of Sichuan, and in their village there's no red line to indicate what will be inundated by the rising river. Nothing—no houses, schools, temples, or any living thing—will remain above the water. When it's their turn to leave, Xia Yunquan, his wife, and another 635 neighbors follow the government's orders and gather on the docks of the city of Chongqing, laden with their belongings. Sobbing, one by one they climb onto an old steamboat, which soon weighs anchor and heads downriver. The boat moves slowly, and the Xias are acutely aware of floating farther and farther away from the courtyard where they kicked a soccer ball for the first time, the tree where they first kissed as teenagers, the restaurant where they got married, the place where their daughter took her first steps . . .

The boat crosses the heart of China, leaving behind the Three Gorges, Qutang, Wuxia, and Xiling, the landscapes that Chinese poets and painters have described so often in words and in watercolors. It keeps sailing down the Yangtze until the river meets the ocean in Shanghai. The residents of Yunyang are taken to a small island called Chongming in the mouth of the river, where the government assures them that they will be starting a "new and better life." The Xias arrive at their destination after a long journey and find an unfurnished, unheated house in the middle of nowhere. Their neighbors have been scattered throughout fifteen different provinces to prevent mass demonstrations. With no glimmer of their old life to cling to, the Xias are engulfed by an overwhelming emptiness. They want to go home. Before them, dazzling, Shanghai: the new China on display. The city rises up like the landscape of a future world, the financial district of Pudong looking like something out of a science-fiction movie and the tops of skyscrapers disappearing into clouds of pollution. The highways wind through the city, lit by sky-blue lights; there they go, in their BMWs with tinted windows and mistresses on their laps, the dreams of Mao's egalitarian society. Shanghai looks different to each of its inhabitants, so it's no contradiction that the Xias want to leave as soon as they arrive and most Chinese want to get there as soon as possible. No contradiction, either, that for the Xias this is the place where their dreams end and for the Yangs the place where theirs begin.

Several years have passed since my last visit to Chaojun, but the Yangs' new home in Shanghai is easy to find: you can follow the notes of the piano that spill out the windows and sweep down the street just as her music slipped down the halls of the Little Emperors Palace the day I met her. The family has moved, leaving the home where they invited me to have tea and listen to Chaojun's playing one spring afternoon. The Yangs used to live in an old one-story house in Jing An, a neighborhood that has been gradually hemmed in by shopping centers and new buildings, one of those places where the two Chinas, old and new, coexist in the same square kilometer. On one side of Nanjing Road were the large display windows of the Plaza 66 shopping center with the latest styles from Chanel and Louis Vuitton. On the other, down the alleys only a hundred meters away, the Yangs and their neighbors lived in tiny houses, waiting without complaint for the eviction notices that would inevitably precede razing their homes to make room for new apartment buildings and shopping centers.

Since when has protesting been an option in a dictatorship?

Old things are identified with poverty for the emerging Chinese middle class, and the country has decided to erase its past—old and poor—and build atop its ruins. There's no room for sentimentality. China inspires great admiration in people when they look only at its economic development and disregard the damage caused by its instantaneous rebirth, which has been driven by an urge to make up for lost time: enormous new cities with as much soul as the cement they're made of; populations that never see the sun, which is hidden behind a cloud of pollution; a society in thrall to the new religion of money, where everything else has ceased to matter. Confucianism's respect for hierarchy in this new China has been transformed into a ladder on which everyone has an eye on the rung below him and people with a little bit of power step on those who have less, while the latter tread in turn on those further down who have still less. One day the Chinese will look at themselves and wonder if there wasn't another way to put behind them the past from which they fled so hastily, eager to embrace a future that they no doubt deserved. In the meantime, stubborn residents who refuse to be evicted from the neighborhoods that real estate sharks consider most desirable are summoned to the Party headquarters by corrupt officials on some pretext—come, let's discuss your situation, we'd like to help you. When they get back home, their houses have been reduced to rubble. Their lives, demolished.

The Yangs' new home is barely forty meters square, but they've arranged it so there's room for Chaojun's old piano. If they'd left it behind, they'd have had to leave their dreams, too. A wealthy businessman who has decided to sponsor the little girl helps with the rent. Every month he also provides a little money so Chaojun can keep taking lessons. The little prodigy is now twelve years old. She continues to play the piano, giving concerts around China and sometimes traveling abroad. The girl still does not charge money for her performances, and it has become harder and harder to bear the economic burden of her journey toward success, with constant trips to enroll her in contests and more lessons. The family survives on Yang Weiqi's tiny $120 monthly retirement pension. His wife,

Zhu Li, says that the three years since we last saw each other have been difficult, and they now fear for Chaojun's future. "The pension doesn't provide enough money, and I don't have a job. We need money if Chaojun is going to move forward in her career. Otherwise, who knows what will become of her?" Zhu Li says.

These doubts have begun to gnaw at the Yangs. Chaojun is still an exceptional pianist, but is she good enough to make up for her parents' sacrifices? It's too early to say, but the Yangs' expectations have grown over time, and it's no longer enough that their daughter be better than a man. They hope to make her a star, and the possibility that that dream will remain unfulfilled weighs on them. The fame, the car, the house, and the leap to the middle class would fail to become a possibility. When I ask her about her biggest achievement in the past few years, Chaojun reminds me of her concert in Paris in 2003, of the audience's applause and the politicians in attendance. "That day, I knew I wanted to be a pianist," she says. The Yangs are convinced that in order to achieve her dreams, the girl must go abroad, where the Chinese musicians who've gone the farthest completed their studies. They ask me if I know of a scholarship, perhaps a European conservatory.

"If only we had the money," Zhu Li sighs. "We've never wanted Chaojun to be successful so that we could have money; we wanted her to have the money and build a future for herself. But we've always believed that if she did become a great pianist one day, she'd pay her parents back for the sacrifices we've made to help her succeed."

Nobody can say exactly if Chaojun will eventually stagnate as a musician. During her first few years of lessons, she absorbed her teachers' explanations easily and repeated her exercises with precision. She could practice for hours. She never complained. Now that she'd perfected her technique and it was time to take her music a little further, living in China was becoming a handicap. The violinist Isaac Stern visited the country in 1979, invited by a regime that wanted to revive music. When he returned to China a few years later, he found that many of the child prodigies whom he'd heard in the Shanghai Conservatory of Music, and who had impressed him so much on his first visit, had stopped progressing. Once the little Chinese musicians got to a certain age, they had a hard time moving forward.

Shortly after I met Chaojun, I was given an explanation for this problem during a visit to Zheng Quan's violin-making workshop in Beijing. Zheng Quan was a musician who had been persecuted during the Cultural Revolution and survived the purges to become one of the greatest luthiers in the world. Zheng explained to me that Chinese education focuses a great deal on technique and practice but fails to nurture imagination, improvisation, or creativity. In its fear of developing independent minds, the Communist Party had exacerbated this mechanical, monotonous approach to learning. The foundation of the party's hold on power, after all, lay in the idea that the regime would take care of the thinking, while citizens had only to follow along like sheep. China was now building dozens of auditoriums, manufactured more pianos than the rest of the world combined, and had twenty million students who, just like Chaojun, were trying to become stars. And although only a few would make it, their success seemed to be less a question of innate virtuosity than one of quantity, the inevitable outcome of the law of probability for a generation that had embraced music like none other in Chinese history. What had happened to all the others left behind, despite the time they'd devoted, the sacrifices they'd made?

"We Chinese aren't very good at expressing our emotions in public," Zheng told me. "And what is music if not expressing emotions, the same as any other way of expressing them?"

The day she played for me in the house in Jing An, I'd asked Chaojun what she felt when she was at the piano. "I don't feel anything, I just play," she'd told me. Zeng would say that the same thing was happening to Chaojun that Stern had seen in the other conservatory students who had stagnated in the Chinese system. As children they made rapid progress and became skilled pianists. But when it came time to express themselves through music, they couldn't do it, partly because they'd been trained to restrain their emotions and not venture beyond convention in their thinking. They hadn't been taught to follow the music. I wondered whether many of these young musicians simply lacked something essential to create and to develop as artists and as human beings. Freedom.

A few years would pass before I got news of Chaojun. She had moved to the United States, to enroll in the Interlochen Arts Academy before being offered scholarships from thirteen music schools across the country. She was to play in a fundraising concert in Voorhies Hall, Bay View. As I looked at her picture in a local newspaper, her fingers gliding across the keyboard, she reminded me of the little pianist I once listened to playing at the Little Emperors Palace in Shanghai. Now, an eighteen-year-old woman, her dream seemed closer than ever. On her big night, Chaojung was going to play Bach's second prelude.

"It's my favorite," she had told me the very first day we met.

I've long been convinced that the hardworking, entrepreneurial character of the Chinese people means that the country is destined to be a wealthy place, even if it stumbles along the way and is still plagued by power-blinded leaders. But the 157 Chinese emperors, the nationalist leaders Sun Yat Sen and Chiang Kai Shek, and even Mao himself, who despite his railing against the past was just another Son of Heaven, emperor number 158—all of them had sought something more than riches for their people. They were convinced that they belonged to a superior race, one destined for greatness. The new leaders are no different. They ask their people to aspire to that greatness but deny them the freedom with which to develop the creativity, humanity, and independence that make greatness possible. Communism without equality, capitalism without freedom. China is advancing spectacularly, but it has failed to establish the foundations of a just judicial system, strong institutions, an open civil society, or an economic model that gives equal opportunities to its citizens.

A country cannot achieve greatness when it imitates, only when it is imitated. A country, to be great, must inspire others. A country can only be great when it has built a society capable of thinking and developing independently, when its history is based on the truth and its present is inspired by its people's rights. Greatness is incompatible with the executions in recent years of thousands of prisoners, almost always without proper judicial oversight, and the subsequent harvesting of their organs for transplants. Greatness is incompatible with the use of psychiatrists to lock up political dissidents who suffer from what regime doctors describe in their reports as "reformist hallucinations," "political monomania," "religious excess," or "excessive interest in foreign trends." After all, wouldn't a person have to be insane to oppose a regime capable of treating its citizens like that? Greatness is incompatible with the occupation of Tibet and the obliteration of its culture, and with the execution of unarmed students on the streets of Beijing. And no, there is no greatness in the destruction of millions of dreams, sacrificed not for the common good but for the greater glory of the new emperors and their second Great Wall, the Three Gorges Dam.

On a trip to the village of Changle, in the coastal province of Fujian, I came to understand the degree to which dictatorships pervert societies. It was June 2000, and the corpses of fifty-eight Chinese immigrants had just been found in the British port of Dover; they had suffocated inside a freight truck while attempting to come to Europe. Although China was now a land of opportunities, some young people still believed that their future lay in Europe, the United States, or Australia. In some villages, eighty percent of the inhabitants had emigrated. In Cang Xa, population 300, I met the families of two of those deceased in Dover. The day before, the village had wept for its dead and the Hong Kong press had published photographs of mothers fainting with sorrow. They had watched their sons and daughters leave with traffickers who'd promised passage on a freighter transporting silk, with air conditioning and beer and food for all. For weeks the would-be immigrants lived in darkness in a rusted shipping container thirteen meters square, with hardly any food, until they reached Holland. There, they were crammed into a truck until their oxygen ran out.

When I arrived in Cang Xa, the same mothers who the day before had been shattered by the loss of their children now looked serious but whole. Some were smiling. I tried to interview them, but they insisted that they had no child who had left for Great Britain, much less one who'd broken the law by deserting the great mother country. On the way out of town, a sign warned: *Abandoning your homeland is dangerous and illegal.* I couldn't make sense of it. Hours earlier, these same people had been sobbing disconsolately, but now they seemed like somebody else entirely. I was leaving when a neighbor's whisper explained everything: "The police have been here."

The authorities had visited Cang Xa a few hours before I arrived and ordered people not to talk with the press and to deny any news about deaths in the town. The inhabitants' pain had disappeared, hidden behind their fear of the regime. Happiness and sadness, too, were the property of the government. The brutal, invisible power of the dictatorship was apparent. Omnipresent. Infallible. The Party had declared: Your children are not dead. Do not weep. And the people of Cang Xa no longer wept for their children.

Sooner or later the day will come when China lives in freedom; it may even come while this book is being published. I am certain of it, and my certainty is based not on politics or economics but on the conviction that a Chinese journalist's aspirations are the same as my own; that a mother from Cang Xa and another from Norway feel the loss of a child the same way, whether they weep or not; and that the dreams of a peasant from Shanxi are not so different from those of a rancher in Texas. One not-so-distant day, this one-fifth of humanity that still lives without political freedom will no longer fear a call from the Public Security Office police in the middle of the night. China will have the opportunity to reconcile with its past and proudly seek whatever future it chooses. Its people's determination and willingness to sacrifice will be fulfilled by the emancipation of its creative, independent spirit, and thousands of Chaojuns will seek excellence far beyond the limitations of a single way of thinking. When that long-awaited day arrives, China will at last have achieved greatness.

Man Hon

My first apartment in Hong Kong, when I arrived in the city as a correspondent in October 1998, was a small studio thirty-five meters square on Old Bailey Street. It received regular nocturnal visits from the rats and was located across from the old Victoria Prison, so that from my window I could clearly see the yard and the prisoners, most of them illegal immigrants who had come to try their luck in the Pearl of Asia. I could watch them exercising, huddling in circles to discuss their misfortunes, and sometimes, more out of boredom than anything else, organizing a minor riot to protest conditions in the prison, which had hardly been renovated since the British first built it in 1841. Hemmed in by the chaos of the big city, amid restaurants, bars, and skyscrapers, the little jail fought not to be torn down and turned into another shopping center. A sign on the main wall announced the institution's rules: prisoners were forbidden from escaping; outsiders were not allowed to park their cars next to the prison walls. That bachelor pad where I spent my first year as a correspondent had plastic cutlery, a perpetually empty refrigerator, a pair of old sheets at the windows playing at being curtains, a wooden desk rotting with humidity, and a liquor cabinet. It was a rat-trap, but for a young reporter ready to take on the world, it had all the charm it needed. The paper had just opened the correspondents' office, and I wanted it to cost them as little as possible, at least until I'd convinced my bosses that it had been worth taking the chance.

When I returned from East Timor a newlywed, Carmen and I moved to an apartment at 31 Seymour Road, which had spectacular views of Victoria Harbor. Given its role in ruining my honeymoon, the newspaper couldn't refuse me the higher rent. The apartment was in one of the city's more than seven thousand skyscrapers, up in the hills, so high that from my office I could watch the eagles of Hong Kong in flight. Sometimes they sped straight toward my window until all at once they wheeled in the air and disappeared among the skyscrapers. I spent two years trying to capture the image of one of those magnificent birds in the moment just as it looked like it was going to crash into my office, but I always picked up the camera too late or the eagle swooped out of the frame at the last second. I left that apartment without ever managing to take that photo and installed myself in my last apartment in Hong Kong—I would eventually move to Bangkok—next to the Chinese Christian cemetery in Pok Fu Lam.

And so I replaced the whirlwind of living in downtown Hong Kong with the serenity of the dead. The birth of my children had changed everything, and it was the perfect place to take walks with them in the afternoon. Ricky Tam was always wandering around the cemetery, hard at work carving, with surgical precision, the Chinese characters of families' farewells on the gravestones of their loved ones. Ricky thought we were a little crazy, "these *gweilos* [foreign devils]," because, unlike him, we had no reason to live next to the dead.

"It's a tranquil place in a stressful city," I told him once in an effort to explain why I liked it.

"Yes, it's very quiet," he answered. "Except when they get angry."

"Who?" I asked.

"The ghosts of the dead," he said with a mischievous smile.

The Pok Fu Lam cemetery is deserted for much of the year, with hardly any visitors except on the special holidays marked on the calendar, days on which the living surpass the dead in number. On those days, hundreds of Hongkongese can be seen marching between the graves, which are arrayed in perfectly straight lines, each with a black-and-white photograph of the deceased embedded in the tombstone. The busiest holiday, the Chung Yeung festival, takes place on the ninth day of the ninth lunar month, when the Chinese come to honor their dead. One of the traditions consists of burning objects to send as gifts to the dead in the other life. You only have to walk through the cemetery during the ceremony to take the pulse of the city and confirm once more that no other culture is more focused on material wealth than the Chinese. People light wads of fake bills, because there's no reason to think that life in the other world is going to be any cheaper than here among the living. They burn cars—a toy Ferrari or Rolls Royce—understandable in the city with the most luxury cars per capita in the world. They burn all kinds of houses, small and large, because nothing is more venerated on this crowded island than the square meter. And during unusually hot summers, many burn miniature replicas of Hong Kong's true obsession: air conditioning. Those who have ended up in hell will certainly appreciate it.

Money, cars, magnificent houses, and air conditioners. Of course none of it existed 150 years ago, when Hong Kong was a poor village in a forgotten corner of the South China Sea. In that insignificant port, the British found a base from which to numb the Chinese with the opium trade, which the East India Company sold in exchange for silk, silver, jade, spices, and other Oriental treasures. One version of history, which is always a draft of itself, claims that a Qing official, Lin Zexu, decided to end the trade with foreigners, tossing a large cargo of twenty thousand crates of opium into the sea, unaware that his audacity would open the doors of China to the world. The English seized on this affront as an opportunity to sink the shabby local armada, march on Nanking, and happily accept as their spoils the island of Hong Kong. The territory was originally ceded to London in perpetuity, but in politics, as in life, nothing is forever, and on October 1, 1998, when I landed in Hong Kong for the first time, thousands of people were celebrating National Day, a holiday in honor of communist China, which a year earlier had regained sovereignty over the British colony.

Gazing upon what is probably the most spectacular cityscape in the world, with the illuminated skyscrapers of Central, Admiralty, and Wanchai soaring above the "fragrant harbor," it is difficult to imagine a better deal than the one Deng Xiaoping scored for

China. Beijing ceded an insignificant, sparsely inhabited rock—and reacquired the New York City of the East, the city of dreams and money, one of the few places in the world where a person can wake up penniless and go to bed a millionaire. Or vice versa. All those skyscrapers, which huddle so close together that sometimes it feels like you could reach out the window and touch the building next door, rise up out of the most unexpected places, immense symbols of power and money. Hong Kong, with its mix of East and West, its old ramshackle Chinese houses dwarfed by glass skyscrapers, the steam that carries the smell of noodle soup out of the restaurant kitchens, the traditional cobbler and the necktied executive working on the same street, the chaotic neighborhoods and the dark, dirty alleyways, the noise of construction and the organized disorder of the bustling crowd on Queen's Road—the sum of its many uglinesses makes Hong Kong a strangely beautiful place.

For a long time, the city was an oasis in the middle of an uncivilized desert for thousands of Chinese who fled first the Japanese occupation and then Mao's political dysfunction on the Chinese mainland. But its doors were closed. Hong Kong was the forbidden dream. Thousands reached it by boat or crossing the border at checkpoints such as Lo Wu, the frontier of dreams. The newly arrived first crowded into poor slums, but over time the government built housing for them and the commercial instinct of the Chinese people, freed from the shackles of mainland communism, took care of the rest. Today, most of Hong Kong's population is made up of those immigrants, their parents, grandparents, and descendants. They began a race for success, and from the beginning it was clear that not everyone could win. The lack of space, the brutal competition, and the hardships of the city made the new Hongkongese tough, and they swore they'd never look back. Little by little, the city became more business-oriented, more prosperous, more efficient, and less human, a paradise for the entrepreneur and a cesspool for the weak.

Some were lucky, like Li Ka Shing, who arrived in Hong Kong when he was twelve years old and today is one of the wealthiest men in the world. It's impossible to live in Hong Kong without expanding the Lis' bank account. Any supermarket you shop in has a fifty percent chance of being owned by the Li family; if you turn on the light, the Lis' utility company will send you the bill; buy a house, and you've probably got a mortgage that makes the Lis a little bit richer.

Others were not so lucky. Peter Zheung arrived in Hong Kong when he was twenty, and today he has nothing. He lost his job as a waiter after losing one of his legs in a fire. With no money and no way of surviving, trapped in a society that has no time to take care of the people who fall behind, he's ended up renting space on the fourth floor of 24 Fuk Tsun Street. The apartment is divided into little cages that form rows three compartments high. All the cubbies are identical: little more than half a meter tall, a meter and a half long, cardboard-lined floor, iron bars, and padlocked shut. Peter is one of hundreds of "cage men" in Hong Kong who go to bed every night by crawling into their pens. And they're grateful to have one, because in a city with hardly any room, there's always somebody else ready to claim their spot. Sleeping beside Peter is his neighbor, Mr. Tong, who never leaves the door of his cage open for fear that somebody will steal his belongings: an old suitcase, an alarm clock, and a box of cookies. He looks like a bird, crouched there with his arms around his knees, as if he's adapted to the gloomy human aviary where he lives.

"You know something?" Peter said to me the day I met him, soon after my arrival in Hong Kong in 1998. "My wheelchair and I haven't left this place since I got here two years ago. I'm afraid that if I leave they'll give my cage to somebody else."

Yes, the race to make it, the same one that China is now running, has sapped Hong Kong's humanity. The city is now an immensely rich place. So why do I feel like it's also such a sad one? The feeling first hits me when I see the faces of the Hongkongese waiting in the arrivals lounge at the airport, and it's reinforced when I pass down its cramped thoroughfares in the taxi taking me home and see them walking, serious and sunk in thought, as if carrying a great burden. To find happiness and *joie de vivre* in the city of money, you have to wait until Sunday, when thousands of Filipino service workers take the day off and invade the downtown, enlivening it with their dancing, food stalls, and laughter. It is strange that the people who should supposedly be the most miserable seem the happiest, and those who appear to have it all look wretched. The Filipinos are often forced to sleep in tiny rooms, if not on the kitchen floor. They have left everything behind to educate other people's children. When bad times arrive, they watch the government cut their salaries, already the lowest on the island, so that Chinese families don't have to give up their servants. They are sacrificing their lives so that their children don't have to sort through other people's garbage in the Promised Land. Yet they are the joy in a gray city. In all the surveys on global happiness, regardless of their scientific validity, the Filipinos are considered among the happiest people in the world. The residents of Hong Kong score among the lowest. Despite poverty, injustice, corruption, war—think of something bad, and the Philippines have it—and the way the magic of the seasons punishes the islands, most Filipinos describe themselves as "very happy." The Centre for Research on the Epidemiology of Disasters may have deemed the country the one most affected by natural disasters in the world, but Filipinos help each other out, share good and bad, enjoy their families, nurture and maintain strong social bonds, and are able to be content with very little. They know poverty in the Promised Land, but nobody's ever heard of loneliness.

The people of Hong Kong, on the other hand, live trapped in perennial dissatisfaction. They need to feel like part of the city's success, so eleven days of vacation a year are enough—too many, even—and they work Saturdays, too, without cease. In the downtown area, you don't have to set foot on the street when you go shopping. Most of the shopping centers are connected by walkways between the buildings. The sidewalks are narrow—or nonexistent—if there's no store around. Who would want to walk in a place with no shops? On a trip to Bhutan once I met two Sony technicians who had come from Hong Kong for the launch of the country's first television channel. We were at the top of a hill, with a spectacular view of the Thimpu Valley, one of the most beautiful places on earth, spreading before us. One of the men sighed deeply and I perked up, expecting to hear a paean to the valley's splendor. Instead, I heard a long yawn and a voice saying, "I can't take another day of this place. There's nothing to do here, not a single shopping center."

In Hong Kong, you are what you can buy. It doesn't matter whether you're going to use what you buy or whether you need it, just that you can buy it: your trips to the shopping center are what determine your social position. That's why a Tai Tai (the Chinese colloquial term used for a wealthy married woman who does not work) and a secretary both go to Tiffany to buy the same piece of jewelry. For the society dame, the bauble costs a pittance, while the secretary is willing to eat in the cheapest restaurant in the city every day and spend months of her salary to own it. Nothing is too expensive if it can be shown off. In a city with so many opportunities, is there a bigger failure than not grabbing hold of one as it speeds past?

I wonder if, in its incredible—and admirable—journey toward progress, something has gone terribly wrong with Hong Kong. In its extraordinary transformation from insignificant fishing village to Asia's financial hub and a symbol of economic power, the Pearl of Asia has buried its soul beneath a massive shopping center. The city has reclaimed land from the sea, dumping tons of cement into the harbor so it can keep building new developments, new buildings, new shopping centers. This is a place where a bit of green space has never won out over a big real estate deal. Hong Kong will do anything to earn more, a little more, a lot more. To buy more, a little more, a lot more. Even if it means living less, a little less, a lot less. The city has become hard, selfish, and indifferent.

Yu Man Hon got lost in its indifference.

August 24, 2000: Man Hon is pretending to run away from his mother. He's played this game before: the boy runs a few meters away, just far enough to feel separated from Yu Lai Wai Ling, close enough not to lose sight of her, reassured that he can go back to her at any moment. The game ends when Man Hon stops and spins around, laughing, in the distance, waiting for his mother to catch up with him, telling her with his smile not to worry, that he is just fooling around.

Mother and son go up the escalators that lead to the platforms in the Yau Ma Tei subway station. Man Hon moves ahead a few steps, weaving around the people gripping the handrails on either side. He stops for a few seconds, looking back at his mother, who is trying to get by the other people to reach his side. But the escalator keeps carrying Man Hon upward, and other travelers are blocking Mrs. Yu's way. The boy disappears from his mother's view as he arrives at the platform.

"Man Hon, stay where you are! Don't go anywhere!"

A train pulls up right at that moment, the doors open, and Man Hon decides to keep playing. He steps into one of the cars, the loudspeaker announces the next station, and the doors close. Mrs. Yu reaches the train and tries to catch sight of her son through the windows, begging for somebody to open the doors. But the train has pulled away.

Man Hon is lost.

After their son was born, Mr. and Mrs. Yu—he a government official and she a housewife—thought that their little boy's silences meant that he'd inherited his mother's timid, quiet personality. They didn't suspect he was autistic until he turned three and his brother, one year younger, started saying words they'd never heard their elder son utter. For the next few years of treatment, through endless sessions in special schools and therapies, the boy would only learn to say his name, Man Hon. At fifteen, he had the communication skills of a two-year-old. Physically, though, he was like any boy his age. The Yus accepted that they'll always have to take care of their son: fate had made him one of the weak and he'll never make it on his own. Now that he's lost and alone for the first time, who will take care of him?

Man Hon hasn't gotten on just any train: he's boarded the train of dreams, the one that goes to Lo Wu, the last station. Without knowing it, he is making, in reverse, the journey that for years has brought thousands of Chinese immigrants to the fragrant harbor. Man Hon is headed to a border that no longer separates two countries, marking instead the line that divides a single "country in two systems," the model that Deng Xiaoping promised Margaret Thatcher that China would use to respect Hong Kong's affairs once it took possession of the colony once more.

The autistic boy disembarks at Lo Wu Station and follows the crowd as it moves toward the border checkpoints. Officials on the Chinese side refuse to let him through; convinced that he's a citizen of Hong Kong, they send him back. Hong Kong officials, believing him a mainland Chinese immigrant, handcuff him, interrogate him for hours, and finally, seeing the boy's silence as confirmation of their suspicions, send him back to China. Man Hon is in limbo, trapped between two systems in a single country.

"You don't want to talk, huh?" the official on duty might have asked. "It's lucky for you we don't force anybody to talk on this side, not like the place you're coming from. You've got another system there, you know?"

So Man Hon sobs in no-man's land, hungry and dejected, unsure how to get home again or how to tell anyone what's wrong. Nobody knows for sure what happens next, but somehow Man Hon manages to cross the border to China and enters Shenzhen, the first city you come to on the mainland. Like Hong Kong, Shenzhen was once a small fishing village and, also like its sister on the other side of the border, it has become an ultramodern, consumerist metropolis, a landscape of skyscrapers and gigantic shopping centers. The two cities are joined today by an umbilical cord: Hong Kong businessmen have discovered that the city next door is the perfect place to revive the ancient Chinese tradition of the concubine. In the village of Heung Biling, near the train station, the women in the apartments and beauty salons are supported by middle-aged men who often have a family on either side of the border, both in the same country, each in a different city. When the children of these relationships try to claim the right to live in their fathers' city, they challenge the rigid model that governs the relationship between Hong Kong and China. That model was reviewed in detail by experts in geopolitics and public administration, by politicians and diplomats, but it wasn't designed to accommodate the vicissitudes of the human heart. To what system do the illegitimate children of the border belong?

The massive search for Man Hon in Shenzhen begins several days after the boy's disappearance, when the treatment he's received at the hands of Hong Kong officials becomes a huge scandal in the media.

More than seven thousand police officers start shaking down the city, which is plastered with posters with a photo of the boy and messages asking the locals for help. His mother has written out the text in her own hand: *Lost boy from Hong Kong. Name Man Hon. He's 168 centimeters tall, has all his teeth, is mentally handicapped. Tic: taps his left hand with the index finger of his right hand. Disappeared in August 2000. Now in mainland China. Probably thinner than in the photo, with old clothing or perhaps naked. If anyone has any information that might help us find him . . .*

The Yus can no longer bear the wait in their Hong Kong neighborhood of Lok Fu. The apartment is one of hundreds of cubbyholes in a massive complex that looks like a human beehive. Mrs. Yu decides to move to Shenzhen to join the search for her son in person. Just a few hours after she settles into her hotel room, a man knocks on the door. "I have information about your son. It's no use. Go back to Hong Kong; save yourself the pain and stop searching. Man Hon is dead," he says. The visitor tells her that the police found Man Hon wandering the streets of Shenzhen, took him to a detention center, and tortured him to death because he refused to tell them anything but his name. Like their colleagues in Hong Kong, the police thought that the boy wasn't talking because he had something to hide. They beat him for hours, "It's lucky for you we don't force anybody to talk on this side, not like the place you're coming from." At dawn they carried Man Hon, unconscious, to the hospital, where he died a few hours later. Fearing reprisals, the police ordered the corpse incinerated and covered up any evidence of what had happened.

"Go back to Hong Kong," the man repeats before he leaves. "I can't tell you any more or tell you who I am because I'd put myself in a difficult situation. I just wanted you to know the truth."

Yu Lai Wai Ling decides not to believe the mysterious visitor's version of events. She goes back to Hong Kong and organizes the search for Man Hon from there. It's an impossible undertaking in a country of 1.3 billion people with a surface area fifteen times larger than Spain's. For years she travels all over China, collecting new information, studying maps, and talking with hundreds of officials and police officers in remote cities. So-called witnesses claim to have seen Man Hon with shepherds in Inner Mongolia, in a truck heading west, on the train to Beijing, and even in Tibet. Some say he's been the victim of an organ-trafficking ring, others that he joined a criminal gang in Shenzhen, and others still that he's gotten into drugs and is living in the slums in the city of Guangzhou. Every so often, some opportunist calls and offers information in exchange for money. Wai Ling always agrees to meet and shows up for the blind dates, but the other person never does. She's untroubled by the contradiction: that she's discarded the theory of the man who visited her in the Shenzhen hotel room, saying it's impossible, but persists in believing even the wildest tales of anyone who alleges that Man Hon is alive.

More than four years have passed since her son disappeared, but Mrs. Yu is still determined as only a loving mother can be. She has traveled through eighteen Chinese provinces, ten dozen cities, hundreds of villages. She is a tiny, fragile woman, her eyes marked by the hopelessness of broken souls. Most unbearable is the feeling that if only she'd chased after her son a little faster in the Yau Ma Tei station, if only she'd gotten to him before the train carried him off, if she'd only put a stop to that stupid game earlier, everything would have been so different.

Over the years, the Yus' house has filled up, week by week, with the absence of the boy who one day played at getting lost and then wasn't playing anymore. Drawers, cabinets, and alcoves have been emptied out to make room for documents, reports, and photographs related to the search. The apartment has begun to look like a private investigator's office. On the main wall of the living room, the Yus have hung a large map of China where Mrs. Yu marks the cities she's been to, those she still has to visit, and those she needs to go back to just in case. Before she goes to sleep at night, she reviews the notepad and phonebook on her nightstand, which list important contacts in all the major Chinese cities. She has the names and phone numbers of the chiefs of police of half the country.

"It's a really big country," she says, pointing to the map. "Enormous."

A dozen photo albums with photos of the hundreds of abandoned children in Chinese cities are spread out across the coffee table. Most have dirty hair, lost eyes, and torn clothing, but they have survived.

"And even though it makes me sad to see them like this, they give me hope," says Mrs. Yu, "because if they've been able to survive in the street, why not Man Hon?"

Every once in a while, a police officer calls from somewhere in the country to tell her they've found a boy who might be Man Hon. Wai Ling hastily packs her bags and rushes off, but when she staggers into whatever police station has called, she inevitably finds yet another abandoned boy who isn't hers. Before going back home dejected to await the next phone call, Mrs. Yu visits the train stations and shopping centers in the city and puts up posters that are really letters to nobody: her son would never be able to read them, though she's chosen to imagine that he could. "Man Hon, where are you? Mommy misses you so much. Come home soon."

The monsoon season comes and goes three more times, and the government declares Man Hon's case closed, pays the family a fine, and disciplines the officials who ignored the boy at the border and sent him to China. And the more than two hundred thousand people who crossed the border at Lo Wu the day that Man Hon was there sobbing, unsure how to get home? Did nobody stop to help him? This is the land of opportunities: nobody waits for anybody here. Everything is a rush: food is fast, business is fast, weddings are fast— fifteen minutes and the guard at City Hall calls the next couple. You have to make it as soon as possible. Make it to where? It doesn't matter. You have to move forward, keep going, arrive.

The passing years gradually erases the memory of Man Hon in Hong Kong, which has learned to only look ahead. The media remember the autistic boy only on the anniversary of his disappearance. A few journalists show up, ask some questions, publish a short piece called "Man Hon's Mother Still Weeps for Her Son," and for the rest of the year nobody thinks about it again. The seventh anniversary of his disappearance arrives, and the justice system declares the Yus' son officially dead.

"Like I care," says his mother, clutching the last photo she took of

Man Hon the day before he left. "Is my son more dead somehow, just because there's a piece of paper saying he is? I know he's out there somewhere. They told me that the sadness would slowly fade over time, but the more time passes, the more I miss him, the more clearly I remember him, and the more strongly I feel the need to find him."

Man Hon is still alive, at least in the Yus' home. The bed is made, with clean sheets and a folded pair of pajamas under the pillow, as if they were expecting him to spend the night. And on the bedspread, a red envelope, symbol of good luck. For the ever-superstitious Chinese, luck can shape a person's destiny; it is what drives our lives. A stroke of luck, born of a particular combination of numbers or the orientation of a house, can change everything, for good or for ill. That's why the island's millionaires pay a fortune to reserve a lucky number for their cars' license plates, and why nobody even considers building a skyscraper without having a feng shui expert assess the site to take advantage of universal energy and harmonize all the spaces to ward off ill fortune. Pregnant women will induce their own labor so that their babies will be born in an auspicious year; people put off weddings to a luckier date to prevent early widowhood. The Chinese believe in luck more than anybody else, and I've always found it strange: I see a contradiction between their huge capacity for hard work and their superstitions, between their tendency to push resolutely toward their goals and their conviction that, in the end, the future can be decided by the position of the moon. Could a red envelope on the pillow achieve what years of searching had not, and bring Man Hon home again? Was it not possible that the mysterious man who visited Wai Ling in a hotel in Shenzhen had told her the truth, that all her efforts had been in vain? Or had it all happened the way his mother had imagined it so many times in her dreams?

Maybe, she thinks, that day, at dusk, as the last Hongkongese crossed the border on their way home, one of the Chinese immigration officials had found Man Hon huddled under one of the tables in the restaurants on the third floor of the train station and decided to take him to his bosses. Hierarchies matter in China; nobody makes a decision without consulting a superior, not even a superior.

"Still here?" the official in charge would have asked. "If you talk now, we'll give you something to eat. Where are you from? Who are you? Where are your parents?"

Giving up, eager to go home, the supervisor then ordered the agents to let Man Hon through to avoid having problems when the shift changed. The boy crossed to the other side. Once in Shenzhen, he wandered for days, living on scraps from restaurants and charity from the Chinese nouveau riche, until a group of street children took him in. He joined them. Every year, in the anticrime campaign Strike Hard, the Chinese government gathers up the little delinquents and takes them out to the countryside, where it needs cheap labor to build roads or work on large construction projects. And so Man Hon was sent to pave the highways of the new China, and later he found work in Shanghai, building skyscrapers where people no longer dream of crossing the border to the fragrant harbor, because now China is the place where anything is possible, the setting in which the next race for success has begun. Remember, not everyone can win. There's no time to look back, stop, live. And maybe Man Hon worked in construction for a while and, then a full-grown man, ended up joining a merchant ship, crossing the South China Sea, and traveling, always silent, through the ancient towns of the Far East that are rising up again now, clamoring for a place among the countries that matter.

Yes, perhaps that is the way it had all happened for Man Hon.

The Yus' strength in their tireless search for their son was part of the same spirit that I had found so many times in Asia, a continent accustomed to tragedy as an ineluctable part of life, whose nations are molded by tribulation and the will to get back up over and over again in order to keep moving forward, driven by their people's relentless capacity for sacrificing the well-being of the individual for the sake of the group. It is the spirit of the inhabitants of the Promised Land and their struggle to turn their city of garbage into a decent place to live; of the Afghans and their tenacity in the face of so many brutal wars that are simply part of a single, interminable war; of Chinese society and its search for its place in the world. It is the spirit I found in the East Timorese people as they resisted the

Indonesian occupation with a dignity born of having vanquished fear; it is that of the Korean refugees ready to defy Darkness and risk their lives fleeing in search of Light. It is the spirit of the Indonesian students facing down tanks on the streets of Jakarta in defiance of a single way of thinking, sacrificing their tomorrow for a democracy that many of them would never see with their own eyes.

When I return from any of these places, I often find that I'm studying myself, examining my reactions, wondering whether I possess some of the spirit of the people I've met on the road. Before I even have time to adjust, people's minor problems—their mortgages, their jobs, their weighty decisions on where to go for their next vacation—begin to horn in on the tragedies of those who have lost everything to war, poverty, or natural disaster. I can eat breakfast in war-torn Afghanistan and dinner in wealthy Hong Kong, fall asleep in a plane taking off from a place ravaged by death and wake up in one that's full of life, be transported from the purest abjection to the banality of a Sunday at the mall—honey, which color do you like better? And after each trip I feel like I should keep everything I've seen hidden within me, afraid that what I've experienced will contaminate the tidier, prettier world of those around me.

And like Man Hon, I remain silent.

In time, I feel an irrepressible need to go back and visit once more the courage of the little girl in the pink dress who cheered the spirits of the patients at the Russian hospital in Phnom Penh, the human warmth of the underground children of Mongolia on frozen Ulan Bator nights, the perseverance of Yeshe's endless journey toward compassion in a world often built of small betrayals, and the determination of Man Hon's parents and their loyalty to their lost son. And it is only when I go back that I can look deep into myself and see remnants of that young reporter who left everything behind to travel East, where the magic of the seasons is repeated every year, where the days break first and the Sky God decides which dreams will come true. And which will have to wait for the next monsoon.